Eyebags & Dimples

Eyebags & Dimples

An Autobiography

Bonnie Henna

First published by Jacana Media (Pty) Ltd in 2012
Second impression 2012

10 Orange Street
Sunnyside
Auckland Park 2092
South Africa
+2711 628 3200
www.jacana.co.za

ISBN 978-1-4314-0500-8

Cover design by publicide
Set in Sabon 11/16pt
Printed by Ultra Litho (Pty) Ltd, Johannesburg
Job no. 001921

See a complete list of Jacana titles at www.jacana.co.za

With Love and Gratitude

GREAT GOD AND FRIEND, thank you for all that you have opened my eyes to, as well as all I am yet to see. I can hardly wait. I love you.

Sisanda, your audacity pushed me out of the boat and dared me to walk while holding my hand through the darkest storms – you always said I could do it. Thank you for fighting for me. You are a warrior. I love you.

Thabiso, my midwife, your faith in me helped me bring this baby into the world, you've been a comforter and friend.

Thando, you are a gem. Thank you for sharing your talent and wisdom, helping me to excavate my voice.

To Percy "Mapercent Vilakazi", thank you for being you and making room for me in that big heart of yours.

To Mom, Ahile and Koketso, I love you so much. Some of these memories I share might be painful to look at – for that, I'm sorry. I celebrate you as part of my path, my destiny and my heart.

To all the people in this book, I cherish your memory; for all you gave, thank you.

This book is a letter to all the little girls living inside us big girls.

To Micaiah and Hanniel, no one can take our freedom unless we give it away.

Prologue

FOR A LONG TIME I FELT misunderstood by the world. Now I realise that I was the one who misunderstood me. I've had to forgive myself for being so hard on myself and others. I had misguided and unreasonable expectations, and wandered around aimlessly seeking fulfilment in all the wrong places.

Surrounded by books in my childhood, I marvelled at the power of storytelling and its power to nurture and inspire me. And I prayed to God that one day I, too, would be able to tell stories that would influence and inspire others. Yet when I started writing this chronicle, I didn't foresee that it would become a book. I knew only that I had to unpack my overstuffed bag, the weight of which dragged so painfully on my shoulders. I needed to unburden myself, unwrap the suppressed memories and lay out the events that had created them. And I knew writing was the way.

As time trailed on, the pages multiplied and I became afraid. Many times I walked away, shocked at my own audacity for thinking I could do this. But each time the story pursued me, demanding to be told. In taking the first step on this journey, I had awoken a sleeping giant that I couldn't put back to sleep; he began to chase me, to haunt my dreams. I had begun the telling, and the force of this story now refused to let me rest until all of it was told, right to the last full stop.

I've shared parts of my life I never intended to share, parts I've longed to forget. Realising that revealing aspects of the truth could make members of my family uncomfortable has plagued me with guilt. But to truly heal, I must tell *my* story – not that of others.

African culture has always prized secrecy. We veil the truth in order to protect the group; we teach each other to value group safety above the safety of the individual; we cover our wounds for fear of what our neighbours and peers may say. But under such a veil wounds fester, and then we pass them on to the next generation. I cannot bear to see this cycle continue, so I have taken it upon myself to break the silence and let in the light.

What has emerged is the journey of my life – the story of my battle with depression.

In no way is this an attempt to prescribe solutions; only to turn out my pockets and share with you what I've picked up along my life's journey, in the hopes that you may recognise pieces similar to your own, clues to the riddle of your own soul that may help lead you eventually to the oasis you seek. I haven't yet arrived, nor can I even begin to imagine how it might look, but I have passed some important landmarks on this path.

In this chronicle I share what was stolen from me by depression – that silent, ravenous enemy against which I remained powerless because I didn't recognise its existence. I spent many years in denial, trying to conceal the hole in my heart, evading the world's gaze lest my eyes reveal the bareness of my soul, lest acknowledging it would empower it and give it a home. Consumed by self-imposed isolation and loneliness, I sought solace in all the wrong places, wounding my soul ever more deeply. Finally, I reached the end of my tether. And as I cried out for help, I found a God who'd been awaiting my call, longing to embrace me and lead me to rest, inviting me to take my place in the greatest love story ever. And I said yes.

The path to recovery was perhaps even more painful, but necessary. I had to allow the God I didn't know or trust to touch the wounds I'd covered up for so long, wounds I'd grown so good at protecting from any bump or touch by anyone who got close. When salvation came in the form of a tiny daily pill, I didn't even recognise it as the salvation it was, amid all the criticism and indifference from the people I valued, and the loneliness I faced because of black society's dismissal of mental disorders as a Western phenomenon to which black Africans are immune.

In writing this book I have chosen to recognise the gift in my adversity, to dive off this board into the unknown, and open up my deepest secrets to scrutiny. The process was terrifying; every time I sat down to write, I wrote in fear. But this book is a love letter to all who have walked this same road, blind to the stealthy enemy that lurks among our families, churches, schools and workplaces. It's an invitation to have a conversation about what you may have refused to consider or been too fearful to explore; it's an outstretched hand to hold on to as you open your eyes to the help around you; and it's a reminder that you're not alone.

This book is not about religion; nor does it suggest religion as a solution. But if I didn't mention my relationship with God and how instrumental it was in my recovery, I would be robbing you of the core of who I've become in this process. I fully respect whatever you believe or seek to understand. I ask only that as you read, you consider and open your heart to the gently nagging suspicion that help exists, that there's an experience that holds a truth bigger than your present knowledge. There are answers and resources that can overcome this oppression, and free you from the silent torment that steals the life not only from you but also from your marriage, your children, your friends and colleagues; and from future generations – your lineage, your legacy.

My relationships have been some of the greatest casualties of this condition. But how could I recover them? How could I explain to all those I've lost along the way that it had nothing to do with them, that I've finally figured out what was wrong with me? How could I explain my harsh words, my silences, my cold indifference, the way I pushed them away?

I decided first to focus on getting well, to accept and surrender to the process. Part of my recovery has involved surveying how I've handled my relationships, taking responsibility for the ways I've hurt others and myself through these encounters, and apologising and owning my dysfunction in these relationships.

This hasn't been easy. My modus operandi was always to hide my true self, exposing only what I thought would be accepted. In this way I gave different parts of me to different people, switching masks all the time while the true me remained an elusive phantom.

I have hated every moment I've spent depressed, but with time I've even learnt to be grateful for this condition. In the depths of the abyss I encountered a strength I didn't know I possessed, an unfailing love that makes darkness tremble, and a purpose so significant its power sometimes overwhelms me. With this story, I hope to inspire dialogue around issues such as depression, emotional trauma and mood disorders, which are still, unfortunately, subject to social stigma and cultural taboos. I'm not sure why most black Africans are loathe to accept these conditions as legitimate, but after I was diagnosed, it became clear to me that many in my community are affected by them. Its presence goes undetected and untreated, eroding the soul, escalating and compounding to cause widespread destruction of families through abuse, addiction and social dysfunction.

This book is a candle; I pray that its light will illuminate the dark corners in and around you, make visible what is hidden and bring clarity to the path ahead. Despite moments of doubt, whenever walking away from this book seemed easier than the pain of birthing it, a message, a conversation, a nudge or a sign would always send me right back to it.

In the final hours of completing this book, I had an encounter that forever sealed my heart's conviction that I must finish this project and let it live. I was a volunteer in the tea room at church that day, in the ministry team where we welcome newcomers while answering any questions they have. On that day there was a little girl in the group, no older than twelve, whom I'd spotted during the service when visitors were asked to raise their hands. She'd come with an older lady and I'd greeted them both in the tea room. The girl tapped my arm as I stood chatting to a member of the congregation, and it looked like she wanted to ask something. So I leant down to hear what she wanted to say.

'Can you please pray for me?' she asked.

I led her to a quieter part of the room. 'What would you like me to pray for?' I asked.

'I can't think,' she said, touching her temples with her small hands. 'Whenever I'm at school I can't think.'

I knew that feeling so well. To determine the origin of her statement, I asked if someone had perhaps told her that. 'No,' she said, 'I just can't think.'

'Are you a quiet or a talkative person?' I asked her. 'Quiet,' she said. I asked if she was a happy or a serious person. 'Serious,' she told me. Was she sad a lot, did she sometimes feel like crying for no reason, even if nothing bad had happened? She answered yes to both questions. I looked into her eyes, saw her drooped shoulders and lethargic posture, and recognised all the signs. I was seeing myself as a little girl.

Now I knew what to pray for, what to ask God on her behalf. As we closed our eyes I gently placed my arm around her shoulders and became that little girl as I prayed, praying as I would have when I was her age, had I only known what was going on with me. We agreed to meet again the following Sunday to work out a plan to get her help.

This book is dedicated to all those little girls and boys out there, and to those of you who love them. I want to assure you that help is within reach.

1

My Father's House

As any black South African kid can tell you, religion is a constant, gigantic entity in their childhood. For black people, going to church is an essential ingredient of every good person's make-up. Whatever debauchery they may indulge in during the week, as long as they do it discreetly, come Sunday it's all water under the bridge as soon as they set foot in a church. I was no different in that regard.

Like most children, I never really got the point of church, especially because some of the most unpleasant adults were the ones who frequented church the most. For me it was a Sunday tradition in which I took part reluctantly, only because my mother thought it was a first-rate idea. My siblings and I were enrolled in the tradition by our mother, the way mothers enrol their kids in all kinds of activities.

What I hated most about church was the three-kilometre walk to get there every Sunday. My feet and shoes would get caked in dust, and the sight of them brought a lump to my throat and left me in a terrible mood. I hated dirt with every fibre in my body. But no matter how cleverly constructed my excuses were, nothing ever dampened my mother's determination to get us to church every Sunday.

Our church was the Zoé Bible Church, which held its services in the hall of Thaba Jabula Secondary School in Klipspruit. The fact that church was held at a school may have influenced my dislike of it. Still, I didn't exactly hate it. Our charismatic pastor cut a dashing figure, especially in a suit. And I loved staring at his kids. They were so good-looking, with their long hair, immaculate outfits and perfect behaviour. Perhaps I just assumed they were well behaved because they looked so good, or that they were good-looking because they were pastor's kids. If your father was a pastor you surely had no desire to misbehave.

Occasionally, I really focused on what the pastor was saying and sang from my heart. During some hymns the congregation would break into choreographed sequences to match the words – if the lyrics said 'I walk with him and sit with him' the congregation would animatedly mimic walking and sitting. If I managed to not let my awkwardness get in the way, there was a kind of happiness about being at church. But mostly I dismissed all this as silly and unnecessary, a far cry from the composed and discreet behaviour at Mass on Friday mornings at Belgravia Convent, where I attended school until Standard Four. I knew that the nuns would vehemently disapprove of these displays of emotion at church, yet once in a while I'd find myself enjoying some of the catchier tunes.

People came in their Sunday best from all over Soweto to worship and listen to our pastor's engaging sermons. But the start of the sermon was the signal for us kids to go off to one of the classrooms for Sunday school. Our Sunday schoolteacher was very strict and I never dared get into her bad books. But it wasn't difficult as I was a quiet child, something I believed God approved of.

We sat on orange chairs, each marked with the school's initials in peeling black paint behind the back rest. I didn't pay much attention; I simply sat there, and my biggest sin, when I thought no one was looking, was to flake the paint off, leaving tiny pieces of black under my fingernails after church. From the way the school property was vandalised I could tell its pupils were neither fond of it nor disciplined, so peeling paint off the chairs wouldn't make much difference, I decided. Sometimes I wished that I could 'catch the spirit', an experience adults spoke of and seemed to long for, but which was granted only to the holiest of individuals. I figured it would set me apart and mean God was pleased with me.

I didn't speak much as a child. I kept to myself and cringed if any sort of attention was pointed in my direction. I always felt foreign in my own body. I had an awkwardness, a discomfort with my appearance and movement, and my skinniness didn't help. This self-consciousness accompanied me wherever I went, mocking me the way boys on a street corner sniggered at the girls' legs as they passed. This feeling lurked deep and sometimes seeped through my composure to the surface. I can't recall the precise moment that I noticed it; it was there from the first moment I became aware of myself, as if I'd been born with it. It regulated my moods and behaviour, dictating how far I could go, how much I could relax or laugh. My default position was always a subtle discomfort, an uncertainty lurking behind every activity I engaged in; it was a feeling that something wasn't quite right about me and my way of doing things; that I didn't belong.

Kids laughed at me all the time. I realise now that kids are often nasty and revel in the misfortune of others, and sometimes I, too, participated in mocking other kids. But at the time the problem seemed uniquely mine, as if I had a sign on my forehead saying 'Laugh at me'.

Walking home from the taxi stop after school, I got mocked for carrying a hockey stick, wearing a blazer or going to a multiracial school. At school I didn't fit in either – not that I tried very hard to. Everything about me seemed out of place. Kids laughed because my hair wasn't relaxed, because I brought the same lunch to school every day, or because I was thin, especially my legs. They called me Stick Mathambo (stick bones). I took it all so seriously, and their words crushed me.

Worst of all, at home nothing I said, did or achieved received any applause or even acknowledgement. If my mother commented at all, it was only to say, 'You can do better.' I so badly wanted to please her, to wipe away that look of disappointment on her face when she looked at me, but it seemed nothing I did ever could. I longed for the day when I'd give up trying to please her for good, though a part of me dreaded it. The result was a gaping hole inside me. It felt like no one had put much thought into my existence or purpose in this world. I was a poorly thought-out plan and now everyone just had to bear with me, though no one wanted me or took any account or care of me. Not my mother; not even God.

God was a distant watcher guy. With our souls spread out on a big chessboard in front of him, he was moving the chess pieces around just for the sake of it to see what might happen. I was just a chess piece being shoved meaninglessly about. I assumed that he wanted nothing to do with me, though I tried to neaten up or put on airs and graces when I prayed, as one did before those in authority.

Still, I liked Psalm 23 and John chapter 3 verse 16, maybe because our Sunday school teacher forced us to memorise them. In those passages my watcher guy's profile sounded impressive. Yet having given his only son to die on the cross made God sound lonely and misunderstood, almost vulnerable – he still willingly gave his most precious gift without knowing if it would be acknowledged or accepted. And how could he do all those amazing things in Psalm 23 and in John, yet still feel so distant? It was all too unimaginable; I couldn't relate to it on any level. Much like my mother, he must have been a pretty tough parent to please, and no other offering from his son except death on a cross would do – such was my young, naive view. He was a good man back then, I thought, but the things disciple John said my watcher guy did clearly didn't relate to me in any practical way. He certainly wasn't willing to do them in my current situation, and anyway, his promises and miracles looked a bit too extravagant.

Besides, God allowed way too many bad things to happen, and he did it knowingly. At Sunday school they'd taught us that God knew everything before it happened. So he had known black people would be despised for their skin colour, but still went ahead with it. Couldn't he have made them lighter, or come up with a less complicated situation? This question bothered me particularly, because I already despised any form of injustice. He could have made people's lives much easier, it would have been no skin off his back. This was just one of many doubts that cast a shadow for me over his supposedly good intentions.

2

My Mother's House

I WAS FIVE WHEN MY MOTHER became suicidal. From then on the mood in our house was always sombre, the ambience gloomy and void of all hope. I spent much of my time feeling sorry for my mother, wishing I could take upon myself all the pain she was carrying, to spare her from the harshness of the world.

At first only my siblings and I knew about her death wish. Over the years she spoke of it increasingly as the solution to every problem. It became her life, her dream, her promise of paradise. She spoke of it longingly with glazed eyes in the way Christians speak of heaven. It was as if death had become her truth. But her threats plunged me into desolation; the constant fear of losing her loomed over my head like a spectre. And she learnt to wield it as a weapon to coerce us into cooperation.

It took many, many years before I stopped listening to my mother. I stopped because it hurt too much, because after years of threats, I realised that they were just a cry for help and an instrument of torture, whether intentional or not, that she waved in an attempt to force us to join her pity party.

Mom hadn't always been like that. I remembered a time when my mother was happier. She would listen to music, sip red wine, cook exotic dishes and dress in stylish clothes. It was still just the two of us then. Each morning she would take me to crèche before she left for work. I remember her waking me on cold winter mornings with a cup of sweet, milky tea in her hand. She'd wrap a blanket around me like a pyramid, with my head peeping out at the top, and speak lovingly and patiently to me as she pottered around getting ready for work. If she went out of view I'd call to her. 'I'm still here, Nunu,' she'd answer sweetly. Only when I was warm enough from the blanket would she dress me and walk me to crèche.

After crèche, Gogo, my granny, would fetch me. On our way home we'd detour past the house of her friend, Gogo Girly, whose name was no doubt conferred by a white Madam for whom she worked as a domestic. Gogo Girly ran a delectable business from a little table covered with a carpet outside her house, selling *amaChappies*, *amaskoppas*, sugary orange sweets that melted in your mouth and white marshmallows freckled with toasted coconut. Gogo Girly was my favourite because she let me nibble on sweets while she gossiped with my granny.

My grandmother was a tall, svelte woman with a graceful beauty, chiselled features and shoulder-length hair

– rumoured to be from Indian blood. She always seemed so caring and kind, but so fragile that it seemed a passing wind might sweep her away. She had spent her life doing domestic work for Jewish families in the east of Johannesburg, where she learnt to cook Mediterranean-style and passed this skill on to my mother. Not surprisingly, I still love Mediterranean food. I loved my granny and enjoyed our closeness. Gogo told good stories and never seemed to tire of my endless questions, which mostly started with why. We'd sit and fold laundry together and she'd teach me how to iron or plait my hair, and sometimes tell me jokes, though there was often a cloud of sadness about her.

But her relationship with my mother was not a peachy one. Gogo always seemed disappointed in my mother. Both she and my mother shared a detached, distant look that seemed characteristic of the Mbuli women. Whenever Mom was in the room, Gogo's face took on a grimace of disapproval. I never forgot that look, with her eyes all scrunched up in disdain. Soon my mother began to use that same look on me.

I have a jarring memory of my mother coming home from work to find my grandmother ironing in the family room. Apparently unprovoked, my grandmother began to hurl insults at her. Mom ignored her and continued to busy herself quietly around the house, but my granny didn't stop. Her voice grew louder and the insults uglier. Then suddenly she was attacking Mom with the hot iron.

Mom tried to fend Gogo off and grab the iron out of her hand. I was terrified and crying, but paralysed with fear and helplessness. My mother eventually managed to peel the iron handle out of Gogo's bony fingers.

I was five when my grandmother passed away. She was only in her fifties. Her addiction to alcohol had finally closed the curtain on her life story. The addiction had so gripped her that she resorted to drinking methylated spirits when she ran out of money to buy alcohol. And she drank it neat. She must have been self-medicating, trying to deal with some unbearable emotional pain deep inside her. Although I loved my grandmother, I was at peace with her passing because she was such a tormented woman.

A few months later my brother was born, and soon Mom began speaking of suicide.

Ahile was the most adorable baby, with cheeks so plump and soft I often imagined biting into them. I took care of him on weekends and school holidays, and I loved being with him, letting him fall asleep on my skinny little lap. His skin always glowed, because in black homes a baby smeared with Vaseline was a loved baby. Five years later, my sister Koketso was born, a perfect little bundle with smooth cocoa skin. She had such a calming effect on me – and still does. She too often fell asleep in my skinny arms. I took even greater care of her because by then I was ten, apparently ready for more responsibility.

Being the firstborn made me responsible for everybody. I hated responsibility, more so because it was thrust on me like an inheritance. It meant I got beatings on everybody's behalf, even when they were the ones who'd misbehaved. And we all got more beatings than I care to recall.

In our four-roomed Soweto house in Pimville Zone 3, my time was spent doing chore after chore, including the cooking and looking after my siblings. My mother was at work during the day, and like many black moms, she had a fixation with cleanliness. I was expected to keep the house sparkling, and failure to do so resulted in a severe beating. My existence began to revolve around avoiding beatings – it became my greatest motivator.

Our house was second from the corner, opposite the Blue Flame bottle store, a well-known landmark. It was part of a strip of shops that serviced a large part of the neighbourhood. I always wondered why the bottle store was the largest of all the shops. There were many bottle stores in the township, all well advertised. Later I came to realise that having so many bottle stores in the township was part of the grand, sophisticated scheme of apartheid, designed to choke the life out of black families.

Of the three food shops, my favourite was the one that sold the best *spykos,* or takeaway food, in our zone – their *amagwinya, ispeshelli, amachips, iwhiteliver* and *isnoekfish* were especially delicious. The other two shops sold staples like bread, milk, cool drinks and general groceries, but my mom didn't like buying from them because they were pricier than the supermarkets in town – like the OK Bazaars. So whenever she sent me to the shops it was with a pained look on her face.

But at times there just wasn't enough money to go around. Occasionally, we went to bed without eating, and there'd be only enough bread for my lunch box the next morning, with sandwich spread and a bit of margarine. The other kids' lunches always looked nicer than mine, so I was ashamed and ate it when no one was looking, or not at all. Fortunately, my brother's school supplied him with lunch.

Mom became really sad at these times. 'I'm pulling hard,' she'd say. I hated hearing those words, because it felt like we might not make it. One day a lady from our church, Lindi Nhlapo, came by while we were eating bread and cabbage for lunch. A little later she returned with a bag of groceries. I learnt the power of kindness that day, and never forgot that generous gesture.

Mom carried a lot of responsibility, and often lamented

being a single parent as she did chores around the house. But she was resourceful and creative with the little she had. She had a cottage at the back of the house, and transformed the garage beside it into another cottage. We called them the back rooms, and rented them out to other families. We often grew close to our tenants, and if they had children I played with them. Ngwana and Ida were the couple who rented from us the longest, and I loved Ngwana. He had a great sense of humour and was always telling jokes. Sometimes he bought me sweets and tickled me as I tried to reach for them, and sometimes I daydreamed that he was my father, and played out imaginary scenes of us doing father-and-daughter stuff together. In these scenes I was always laughing.

But then Mom had a fallout with Ngwana. I was heartbroken when he and Ida moved out. I had few friends, and at that time Ahile was still too young to play with me.

Mom tried to keep me as untouched by my environment as possible, and I was never allowed to play beyond our back yard. If I took too long at the shops I got yelled at and interrogated. She drummed into my head that no one was to be trusted. People were mean, jealous and only wished us the worst. Like most families, she also feared witchcraft, and spoke of how easily one could get bewitched in Soweto. Women gossiped endlessly about the latest victim and the suspected sorcerer, and I found these conversations fascinating.

I longed to be connected to the vast and unknown world out there, but Mom built a strong case against it. So I grew scared of it. Heeding her advice, I became cautious and impenetrable. There was much to be feared out there; it was the only explanation for Mom's paranoia. Stuck at home and bored out of my mind, I would lie on my back on the grass, staring at random cloud formations and making out shapes of animals and objects; sometimes I imagined that the sky was sending me private messages. I also took to writing stories and reading anything I could find. But I still hated being alone; my loneliness was a constant ache in my heart. All I wanted was to be worthy enough to have someone to talk to, to play with me and care for me, just like other children. But it was a losing battle.

'Mama,' I'd plead, 'I don't like being home alone all the time. I get scared and bored.'

'Don't be ridiculous; I have to work. You expect me to stay home and stare into your eyes all day long?'

After my brother was born, Mom hired a babysitter to stay with us. But the babysitter often covered me with a blanket and beat me with a belt while I cried beneath the layer of wool. I tried my best to keep this from Mom, because I preferred the beatings to the loneliness. But Mom finally found out and fired her.

When Ngwana moved out of the back room, a new family moved in with a daughter about three years older than me, and we began to play together. Jabulile was a strong, stout girl with a big protruding bottom and bullish personality. One day while Mom was at work, she told me to lie down so she could show me something. Then she forced herself onto me, rubbing herself against my pelvis till she moaned and groaned and let out a long sigh of relief. I lay there frozen in shock, afraid to move or say anything. From then on I was afraid of Jabulile, and I was relieved when they moved out of our back room. But for years afterwards I was tormented with feelings of shame, helplessness and self-loathing. I became convinced that I'd deserved what she'd done. I hadn't objected, so I must have wanted it; what other explanation could there be? Whenever Mom beat me hard and called me *isfebe* (whore) for losing my school blazer or forgetting to wash the dishes – things that didn't warrant such a label – I assumed she saw something in me that called for it.

Two houses from ours lived a girl called Puleng, with whom I was strictly forbidden to play. Mom said she was 'fast'. 'If I ever see you with her, *ngizokushaya*! I'll give you a hiding!' But when my mother wasn't home, Puleng often rounded up a couple of kids, including boys, to come and play in my yard. Mom wasn't wrong about Puleng. She always wanted to play grown-up games, and she knew a lot about what grown-ups did behind closed doors. We'd play *umandlwana* (house) and Puleng would always insist on being the mother and picking the oldest boy to play the father. She had a strong personality and narrated as we played. 'It's night-time now, and all the kids must go to sleep,' she'd announce. 'Mother and father are in their bedroom.' We'd all pretend to sleep while Puleng took the arm of the 'father' and forced it onto her waist or even her bottom. She was so daring and knew so much about the world that we all worshipped her and believed whatever she told us without question.

Mom's threats could never dampen my enthusiasm for Puleng's company. Sometimes Puleng would come over and we'd peer out from beneath the lounge curtains, shouting silly insults through the open window at other children passing on their way to the shops. We'd base our insults on how they looked or dressed, like *chiskop* (baldhead), *umubi* (ugly), *mShangaan* (Shangaan) or *uyaphapha* (know-all), or we'd just shout *voetsek* (go away). The insults had to be brief enough for us to drop out of sight before the scorned individual saw us. The objective was to make the insults nameless and faceless, as if they'd appeared out of nowhere. Puleng and I would laugh till our stomachs ached, and our giggling fits often meant that the next insult we tried to hurl got choked among stifled giggles.

One day we took the teasing too far. Puleng suggested that we *zula* (wander around) a bit. We wandered beyond Zone 3 till we reached a *skhanga* (open field) in Zone 4, the one I used to have to walk through to crèche years before. The field was still just rough gravel but no longer so barren; now it had a jungle gym and a *mchichirizo* (slide). While we were happily playing on the *mchichirizo*, an older boy appeared and began playing at the far end of the field. He also looked like he'd unexpectedly discovered this makeshift playground. Then Puleng whispered in my ear. Her plan was to watch from the ground until the boy got to the highest point on the jungle gym, then shout '*Heyi wena, jolinkomo!*' and make a run for it.

I asked her what *jolinkomo* meant. 'Don't be stupid man, I just made it up!' she said dismissively. I thought her insult sounded ingenious – a concoction alluding to a relationship with a cow.

We were giggling so hard we had to recover before we had the energy to shout loud enough for the boy to hear. The first time we shouted loud and clear, he glanced over and chose to ignore us. We tried once more, and then again. On our fourth try, his eyes suddenly zoned in on us like a bull seeing red. And then he came for us.

'*Balekaaaa*! Run!' We ran like our lives depended on it, in torrents of laughter charged with the adrenalin that was now pounding through our chests and veins. Luckily Puleng and I were both good runners. Having bagged a head start by timing the attack when he was at the top of the jungle gym, we managed to outrun him. Once we were quite certain we'd lost him, we stopped to catch our breath, doubled over with our hands on our knees for support.

We soon forgot all about the incident. But, unknown to us, the boy just happened to live on our very same street, only one block to the right. And one evening, with the sun setting in a dusty yellow-and-pink sky and the crickets already singing their lament, Mom sent me off to the shop. I saw him just as I was about to turn the corner and cross over. And he was coming straight at me.

Fear crackled through my body like electricity.

'*Bhi! Ankikhutholanga!* Got you!' he shouted, his hand raised as if to slap me. '*Ngithi angikhutolanga.* I told you I'd get you.'

'*Hayi, aksi yimi.* It wasn't me,' I squealed, my voice cracking in terror. '*Bekuwumngani wami, uPuleng.* It was my friend, Puleng.'

The fiery sting on my face was so sudden and so loud that my vision blurred and I staggered, nearly losing my balance. Through hot tears I watched him walk away, turning one last time to wag a finger at me. '*Uzoyeka ukungijwayela kabi!* That'll teach you for disrespecting me!'

I arrived home crying inconsolably, his fingers clearly imprinted across my swollen cheek. My mother extracted the whole story from me, and promised me a vicious beating if I ever dared to play with Puleng again. And I never did, although I missed her companionship sorely.

3

After School is
After School

Soweto was a tough place. Its malnourished scenery was a
far cry from the opulent suburban world I travelled through
on my way to school. Compared to the lush white suburbs,
it was barren, grim and uninspiring. There were no street
names, pavements, parks or anything that beckoned to the
soul. No beauty inspired one to do or become more, and
this was no coincidence – it was part of the plan. The only
beauty lived in the hearts of its people and in the meticulous
cleanliness of their gardens and homes. The women rose
early to sweep their yards each morning and shine their
stoeps in bright red polish, a testament to their resilience

and determination to to live with dignity and pride.

I was blessed to receive a top education while growing up. We all sacrificed a lot for this. My mother, especially, made great sacrifices to afford me this privilege. Almost everything she had went towards ensuring that we got the finest education available, and for this decision she faced great criticism and chastisement from friends, relatives and neighbours. They regularly commented that she was living beyond her means to try to outdo everyone else; why not just enrol her kids at the bantu schools in the township like others did? But my mother's courage never wavered. She kept her sights on the bigger picture and persevered, depriving herself of everyday comforts and relaxation time to make it happen. Perhaps people weren't so much angry at her for it as afraid to do the same. Who were they, in a country like ours, to want a better education for their kids? Like most black people, they knew their place.

Not my mother. She was a strong-willed woman who lived to defy the word 'impossible'. If she was told she couldn't do something or that it had never been done before, that was her cue to go right ahead and do it. And I inherited that brazen, pioneering, nonconformist spirit of hers. Because of her, I loathe the sight of fear; I strive tirelessly to eradicate it from my life, to face it head on and never let it control me.

In 1984, South African schools were segregated, and most black children were forced to make do with an inferior and deprived form of education. Yet I, at the age of five, was sent to a private school, the Dominican Convent School in Belgravia in eastern Johannesburg. At first I was one of only two black children at the school, and in most of my classes mine was the only black face. This wasn't something that stood out for me at the time, although it had a powerful impact on my socialisation.

This was a traditional Catholic school with a strong religious foundation. The convent rules were stringent, and we weren't allowed to run or even raise our voices in the corridors. Displays of strong emotion were simply not proper; a model student was always composed. Mass was compulsory every Friday morning at eight o'clock in a quaint, beautiful chapel with elegant stained-glass windows and the comforting smell of incense. The nuns were our schoolteachers, and we had confession every Wednesday afternoon, followed by our penance. The specifics of our penance depended on the weight of our sins, which usually consisted of pinching a pencil, talking in class or lying about unfinished homework. We might have to say ten Hail Marys, and then mess around outside while we waited for the others to finish confessing their multitude of sins. It amazed me that our 'Father' had the patience to sit through the same bland confessions week after week. I honestly never knew what to confess in there; it was some of my most earnest waffling about nothing.

Attending this school meant that most of my friends were white. But in the midst of apartheid, our friendships were solid and entirely uncontaminated by racial prejudice, apart from the occasional comment from the nuns intended to put black students in their place: 'Stop behaving like savages'; 'We don't speak black languages in this school'; 'This is not the township'.

My school life created a stark contrast to my home life in the township, an often hostile terrain plagued by rioting, random teargas attacks and stayaways during the last thrashing and kicking of the dying horse of apartheid. Sometimes the security forces would undertake slow, menacing drive-bys through the township in their armoured vehicles, which were called 'hippos'. Perched arrogantly on the top of these hippos they would give us kids their most hostile of looks, and we would stop whatever we were busy with to stare back in defiance. It was a regular drill intended to intimidate us into acceptance, and to keep the yoke of oppression firmly in its place.

For years I wrestled with a silent, gnawing sense that South Africa didn't quite belong to me; it felt like a quiet displacement intended to bully me out of my birthplace and inheritance. We endured several scary nights when two or three armed security men barged noisily into our house around two in the morning. We'd wake up with the biggest fright, my mother and I, while they searched our house, speaking loudly to each other in Afrikaans and strolling through our home as if they owned it, searching for anything and everything, rummaging through our stuff and turning all our things upside down. These midnight raids left us feeling violated and helpless, so grave was the assault on our dignity and privacy. Afterwards, it became impossible not to associate the Afrikaans language with aggression and hostility.

Twice, while I was at the shops for my mother, a cloud of teargas was randomly released into the air, making it impossible to see. Instantly the whole area around the shops became a scurry of confusion as we all – mostly children – scattered like ants before a hosepipe. Teargas stings the eyes like a chopped onion but ten times stronger, burning its way up the nostrils and disorientating the mind.

I didn't recognise at the time how the years of trauma visited on my community jabbed at my self-worth and my sense of collective identity. My will was strong, but in deep, secluded corners I carried the shame of being labelled an inferior. Because of this, I nurtured an unacknowledged hatred of South Africa and all that it represented. And perhaps some of this feeling still lingers.

Many adults, including my mom, would warn us children of how evil and dark the hearts of white people were, how they hated black people and would stop at nothing to see the black nation destroyed. Whites were heartless and not to be trusted. Yet my white school friends were nothing like that. We loved each other. We talked, cried, hugged and laughed together, stood shoulder to shoulder, singing our school song in solidarity. The chasm between my school life and my home life was vast, and I often found myself lost in the divide between them.

One day my mother came home driving a bright yellow Opel Kadett. It was a landmark in our lives. Our neighbours oohed and aahed – and had a whole lot more to say behind our backs. Here was my mother, a single black woman in her thirties in apartheid South Africa, who owned her own house as well as a car. This was so rare as to be totally audacious. But she'd always longed for a car, and had first enrolled herself in a driving school to learn to drive. Now that she'd accepted a second job that required working late at night, she really needed one.

Growing up with such a mother made me into a daring adult too, accustomed to taking risks and going where most in my world wouldn't dare. But back then, I simply enjoyed sitting in the back seat of the car as we cruised and sticking my tongue out or scrunching my nose at the kids playing hopscotch or *umgusha* (rope skipping) in the streets, giggling because they could do nothing about it. But I had to sit very close to the window and dodge my mother's eyes in the mirror, because if she caught me I'd get a hiding.

Soon after my baby sister was born, we rented out our old house and moved to a new development three kilometres away in Soweto. The new house was brand new and much bigger. It didn't have much furniture, but it was full of promise: it had clean carpets, three bedrooms, a lounge, dining area and a kitchen, plus indoor bathrooms for the first time in our lives – two of them!

Both my mother's jobs were at the University of the Witwatersrand – a day job in the Student Affairs Department and an evening job till eleven o'clock on the switchboard at Jubilee, the women's residence. Before my sister was born, when we were scared to stay home alone while she worked at night, she took us to work with her. We'd sit on the floor of her booth, drawing and reading, staring at the maze of switches that she handled like a pro, which thoroughly impressed me. At her work I thought my mother was a superhero. She was smart, stylish and always smelled of potpourri – a timelessly elegant and fearless woman. I admired her greatly, and could sit and watch her for hours. She'd joke with and chat to the girls as they strolled in and out of the residence, or scold them for being out late and trying to sneak boys into their rooms. I loved the smile that lit up her face and creased the corners of her eyes at those times.

But after she scolded the girls – or the boys who came looking for them – she would lecture me about how a girl should behave. Yet all her lectures boiled down to a simple instruction: don't come home pregnant. It was the only sex education she ever gave me. She'd go on and on about how these girls' parents paid so much for them to attend this prestigious university – and she knew, because she fielded calls from parents and students at the Student Affairs Department, some of whom poured their hearts out about their financial burdens.

'Don't think for one second that I'm going to pay all that money for you to go and run around with boys like they do!' she'd rant.

'But Mom, I haven't done anything. I'm not even at high school.'

'Well, don't you dare even think about it!' It seemed that to her I was already guilty.

The best thing about Jubilee, or Jubs as it was affectionately called, was the supper. The dining hall wasn't far from Mom's desk and the smells would waft enticingly past my nose. Along with the students, Mom was allowed to get supper in the dining hall, and my favourite treat was the pizza. I found the students' endless moaning about the food extremely ungrateful as I tucked ravenously into my pizza slice, while the oil from the cheese dripped down my forearm.

Over time, Mom's demeanour steadily deteriorated. With hindsight, I'm certain she suffered from postnatal depression after the births of both my brother and sister. The atmosphere in our house followed Mom's mood, and a slab of impenetrable doom hung in the air. Whenever Mom decided to hibernate in her bedroom and sit life out, I became responsible for running the household, making sure the kids were eating and the house was cleaned.

My schoolwork began to suffer and I stopped caring; the weight of my family was like a wet blanket draped over me, smothering the light inside. School went by in a daze; I hardly paid attention. I was overwhelmingly stressed. The anxiety, loneliness and awkwardness slowly gained on me like thick, black oil seeping into every cavity. I saw no point in trying; there was no hope for my life.

From Standard Three onwards, along with the increasing pressure at home, I became disruptive in class. I was restless, anxious and began constantly acting out, doing things that landed me in detention. I was frustrated and stressed, and never wanted to be at home. I hated my life, didn't trust

23

adults and had no faith in authority, so I rebelled against every rule I was expected to obey. The following year Mom was called in by one of my teachers. She said that my marks and behaviour at school pointed to a deeper problem, and suggested my mother take me to a psychologist. Mom took the words personally; she felt the school was taking a jab at her parenting skills, and chose to ignore their advice.

So I left Belgravia Convent on a sour note, and instead of getting help, I was sent to Marist Brothers, where I completed Standard Five. I passed well and seemed to calm down, although our Maths teacher was a neurotic Scottish woman who treated school like a boot camp. I hated maths and often became so overwhelmed that I would weep quietly with my head bent over my desk.

With the arrival of my brother and later my sister, not only Mom's mood but also her finances took strain, and Marist Brothers soon became unaffordable. So at the end of Standard Five I switched schools again. Greenside High was one of the new Model-C schools, government schools that were now allowed to accept black kids. I was part of the first intake of black children.

The culture at Greenside was very white with a sprinkling of Afrikaans. Some of the kids were outright hostile to black people and proud of it, but most were simply indifferent. For someone like me who'd been schooled with white kids from the start, I found this annoying and childish. But I didn't take it as personally as other black kids did, because I knew enough white people who weren't like that, so I knew it had nothing to do with me. I could live with people disliking me because of my skin colour, but what angered me was their sense of entitlement to vomit their racism into my space.

It was really difficult to fit in with the black girls I met at school; I wasn't versed in the latest street lingo or mannerisms,

I wasn't cool enough. So I found myself gravitating towards the white girls who were more accepting. The black kids called me a snob and a coconut, and mocked everything about me. Understandably, the differences between us were significant. Not only had we been schooled in very different social environments, but I was already awkward and aloof, and used to being outside of the group fold. My two best friends, Katie and Sasha, were white. I got invited to all the white kids' parties, and my taste in music leaned more towards rock and alternative while most of my black peers listened to township pop and rhythm-and-blues. I'd attended ballet classes for most of my primary school life, so I walked with perfect posture, my back straight and my feet turned out like a duck. I played hockey instead of netball – for a long time I was the only black girl who played hockey – and I apparently spoke like a white. Yeah, I was different, and I took a lot of flak for it. But that was the least of my problems, so I never fought to fit in or be accepted by them. Whenever the black kids used their smug, street-smart ways against me, I retaliated using my intellect and knowledge, talking circles around them. This became my weapon.

The social side of school was a constant struggle. The lines between the different groups were clearly drawn and you always had to be careful not to step on any toes. Somehow, with my compulsion to speak up against lawlessness, disorder and injustice, I always managed to put my foot in it. In one incident, a commotion erupted because a classmate's bra had been stolen from the change rooms during Physical Education. It wasn't just any bra; it was Christy's French lace La Perla bra that she'd brought back from an overseas trip, and we'd all been allowed a peek down her shirt the first day she wore it. Now everybody was gathered around as she wept hysterically. Christy was sweet and kind and had never done anything to antagonise me. So, soon afterwards, when I spotted the lacy pattern of her bra under Lerato's shirt, I felt duty-bound to tell Christy.

Lerato was a crass, mean girl with a vast knowledge of boys and how to entice them, which she liked to share at the top of her voice on the 74 bus. She was the ringleader of her group and everyone jumped at her instruction. When Christy confronted her, Lerato gave an Oscar performance, declaring that Christy was arrogant to assume she couldn't afford a fancy bra, and pulled the 'it's because I'm black' card. During the altercation it came out that I was the one who'd told Christy. To say that I was neck deep in horse manure would be an understatement. By second break, news had spread that Lerato wanted my head on a platter, and everybody was scared for me – including me. People were wagging their fingers at me in the corridors, saying '*Ayeye, ayeye*, after school is after school!' I well knew I couldn't win a fight against Lerato, and didn't want to get embroiled in her streetfighting ways. But I was terrified. So with Christy at my side, I reported her to my teacher and, to my enormous surprise and relief, Lerato left me alone after school. She evidently knew she was beaten.

Greenside High was a far rougher place than my primary school had ever been. It was survival of the fittest, so you had to belong somewhere; if you were a stray you were a target for ridicule, like a bleeding antelope before a pride of lions. But my friendships at school kept me going. I spent many weekends at Katie's house in Northcliff, a welcome break from the heavy responsibilities I carried at home. Whenever those weekends came to an end and I had to go home, I would weep inconsolably.

4

Like a Bird

MOM WORKED HARD to raise and provide for us, but the backbreaking work without any support made her resentful and begrudging, so I grew afraid to ask her for the extra money needed for school trips, donations or stationery. If I brought home a letter asking for anything to do with money, she'd fling the paper in my face and yell '*Uthi ngiyithathephi lemali*? Where do you expect me to find the money?'

I'd leave her bedroom feeling hopeless and dejected with no one and nowhere to turn to. Mom became increasingly neurotic and irrational as the years progressed. Everything seemed to agitate and overwhelm her. If I entered her room with my homework diary for her to sign, she'd shout and call me names, and sometimes throw it at me. If I tried to explain that I'd get detention if she didn't sign, she'd shout 'Shut up! I don't care!' I'd walk away feeling hurt and ashamed, tears burning my eyes.

I too began to wish I would die. I fantasised about dying, for surely death was better than this torture that had become my life. I just wanted her to love me, to see me, to be glad that I existed. I craved her affection and her approval, but I had to content myself with beatings – they were her only real engagement with me. Her words were always hard, critical and uncaring, abrasive to my soul. I was convinced she hated me. The mere sight of me irritated and disgusted her, and she'd often say so, her eyes inching slowly, coldly over me in disapproval, her lips curled down, nostrils flaring as though smelling a waft of sewage. '*Suka la phambi kwam. Get away from me.*'

I was certain it was my fault. Clearly I repelled love, and if my own mother felt that way, then surely the world saw it too. I was undeserving of love. After such episodes I would sit in my room and wonder if she was my real mother. What had I done to make her loathe even the sight of me? What was I going to do? What on earth had I done to deserve such contempt? It was in these moments that my heart beat its fists in anger against the ceiling of a silent heaven. Why did people say God was good and loving if he allowed these things to happen? I lived with a woman who hated me and, apparently, she was my mother. I saw myself through her eyes, and I believed everybody else did too. If that was how they saw me, rejection was inevitable, so I rejected them first, pushed them away before they pushed me. I kept everybody at arm's length, and vowed to myself that I wouldn't need anyone ever, not even my mother. I could do it; I could wean myself of every expectation and reliance on her, whether instinctive or learnt. Self-sufficiency would be the shield I wore around my heart.

On the rare occasions when Mom was in a good mood, we would lie on her bed listening to her funny stories, and I'd laugh my stomach into stitches. Then, in the blink of an eye, anger and frustration would blow over her like a tempest; her heart would freeze and she'd chase us from her room. I'd be so angry at myself for daring to think that it was safe, for letting my guard down and allowing her in, for believing. I should have known better by then; I should know that the only thing she knew how to do was to crush me.

It baffled me that this behaviour was so similar to the things Mom had told me her mother did to her; some were in fact identical. She'd related numerous stories of my grandmother's cruel words, and the deep hurt and sadness she'd experienced when her mother treated her with such contempt. Yet here she was, visiting the very same horrors upon me. Why, if it had made her feel so bad, did she want me to go through the same thing? A subtle distrust began to creep into my bones.

I grew to distrust everyone, especially adults. They were never quite who they said they were. I decided that the only way to survive was to completely detach from life, to become unaffected by anything or anyone. It hurt too much to care, to believe, to hope, to need or expect love. No one would catch me needing them again. Sometimes I hated my life so much that death seemed the only way out.

To cope with the ache in my heart, I would write and write and write, and as the words bled out of me, the strength would come to face another day. Mom would often search out my journal and read it. No matter how well I hid it, she seemed to know where to look. I'd come home to an onslaught of insults and accusations based on half-baked theories she'd strung together from the clues she'd found in the pages of my private world.

So she also knew, then, that I wanted to die, yet she chose to ignore it. She never referred to it; only to her own constant desire to die. That was all that mattered. Her suicide threats were often triggered by events that upset her during the day, like a phone call from Greenside Primary reporting my brother's disruptive behaviour and lack of commitment.

My brother was hyperactive and struggled to focus on anything for long, and Mom spent a lot of time in and out of psychologists' rooms trying to get to the bottom of it. He was put on Ritalin for a while, yet his behaviour still worsened with each year. In one incident that nearly drove Mom over the edge, Ahile had opened the cage of a teacher's pet bird, which she'd put outside her classroom for some fresh air and sunlight. He had let the bird escape. The school was outraged. It was a naughty thing to do, and brought on more threats of violence, abandonment and suicide from Mom, but it also spoke volumes about the longing in my little brother's heart – our collective longing – to escape, to be freed from our cage.

5

Imminent Death

ONE DAY, AT A HAPPIER TIME, I sat chatting with my mother, sifting through snapshots of her life. In the photos my mother was a stylish young woman with radiant skin and a slender frame. She and my father looked like they belonged on the red carpet. Mom's eyes lit up whenever she spoke of how handsome my father had been – even his nickname was Handsome. She still loved him, she told me, although he'd beaten her mercilessly in later times, and cheated on her with other women. Hearing this wasn't pleasant, but she always insisted that he'd loved her dearly. She was the one he'd wanted to marry, she said, and she remained his most beloved because it was she who'd borne him a child – me. That's why my name was Bonisile, meaning 'proof', as my arrival had proved that he could bear children.

My father's real name was S'dumo Twala, and I was told by those who knew him, including my mother in better days, that I was the splitting image of him. Although in black society remarking on a girl's resemblance to her father is usually a polite way of saying she's ugly, my father, fortunately, was handsome, and his appetite for life, love of style, and prophetic prowess are his gifts and the legacy he left me.

Mom told me that he used to walk around the township with me bundled in his arms, attentive to my every moan. This was rare for a township man and a sure sign of love, she assured me, because men were macho then, and carrying a baby around could cast doubt on their manliness.

Most mornings before he left for work he would stand at the front door with me in his arms, speaking of beautiful things to come. 'My daughter will be famous and her name will be known across the world,' he'd said one morning when I was four months old. 'She will travel to places I've never known, like London.' That morning, Mom told me, she'd chided him for talking rubbish, never guessing that I would, indeed, fulfil his dreams.

My father never came home from work that night. It may be a simple coincidence, but my mother said I was restless and crying all through that night. In the early hours of the morning she received a phone call. My father had been mugged by unknown men on his way home from work. They had stabbed him to death.

The sparkle in my mother's eyes whenever she spoke of my father reminded me that she'd known happiness, that there had once been a time when she was hopeful and not constantly wishing for death. This was the mother I'd known in my earliest years – beautiful, regal and immaculately dressed, the epitome of style, class and sophistication. In our impoverished surroundings, her beauty and grace had been a comfort. She'd loved to cook delicious dishes from fancy recipe books, and I had looked forward to her every meal. Sometimes she'd even served the food with a glass of wine. 'It's is good for the appetite,' she'd say, offering me a few sips to try to get me to eat better. She had also been a loving person back then.

Now my mom so often forgot the food cooking on the stove that after a while the curtains and carpets smelt permanently smoky. Things that fell apart were left unfixed. Disorder reigned, and, try as I might to keep things clean, I buckled under the growing pressure of just keeping the basics together. With all Mom's financial responsibilities, she never had any spare money to make the house into a home, and there was no beauty to speak of. So I was too embarrassed to invite friends over. Besides, how could I explain what was going on here?

When she didn't feel like dying, my mother loved books. Our home was sparsely furnished and entirely without bookshelves, yet there were books everywhere, as if in place of furniture. Books were stacked in almost every corner of the house. There were so many, they formed towers against the walls, and we used them as coasters or even to squish cockroaches. Books were never more than an arm's length away.

Apart from fiction, many of them were about writing, speaking and social etiquette. Mom encouraged me to read everything there was, whether it interested me or not, and I did. At first it was torture, but slowly reading became a place of solace and safety in which I lived my life through the characters I fancied. Not that there was much else I could do, anyway. On weekends we weren't allowed out, and the gate was secured with a tightly wound chain held fast by a giant padlock. As far as my mother was concerned, weekends were for reading.

Through reading, my imagination grew. It created a parallel universe for me where hurtful words were left behind and I felt safe from pain. In this world of mine I was unaffected, unscathed by all that was going on around me. There was no anxiety and time went by at my pace, because I was in charge – my co-inhabitants in this private world couldn't hurt me. In my small, character-filled universe, I was a good girl and a good daughter to my loving mother. I could do and be anything.

Before I started reading I had felt vulnerable and susceptible to everything. But once I began reading, a layer of immunity started to develop, like an outer skin around my soul. I had more control over what I felt and what affected me. This imaginary world began to extend to my everyday world. Gradually, my small universe began to swallow my reality; I wasn't just reading other people's stories any more; I *was* those other people; their stories became mine. The books around me helped me to cope with the pain and silence of my childhood, and to overcome my feeling of exclusion and loneliness, and as they steadily absorbed me, they also began turning little Bonnie into an actress.

Once I had this parallel universe, I experienced less anxiety when my mother entered the room. But whenever Mom beat us 'like we weren't her children', as she put it, I'd be wracked with despair for my brother and sister, longing to protect them, to place myself between the belt and their thin little frames, to hold them in a safe place where no harm could reach them, the way a kangaroo mother would hide her young in her pouch. The sense of helplessness that muzzled me then still paralyses me today when I hear of abused children. Perhaps this is why I so abhor injustice of any kind, and constantly seek to stand up for the voiceless, the abandoned and the dejected. My passion for adoption surely arises from this deep need.

Yet Mom seemed particularly angry at me and my brother. 'I wish I'd never had you,' she would say. 'You've ruined my life; you've destroyed all my dreams.' And then, sooner or later, it always came: 'I wish I could die and leave you to suffer.' Naturally I came to believe that I was a burden to my mother and, by association, to everybody else who encountered me. My existence, and that of my siblings, was the major reason she wished for nonexistence, which made me, in turn, wish I'd never existed. Being in my mother's presence was a constant reminder that I was a burdensome child who'd snatched her dreams away by simply emerging from her womb, her hopes and aspirations twisted and bleeding in my little clenched fists. I lived with the constant guilt that she wanted to kill herself because of the evil of my very existence.

Mom gradually began to spend more and more of her time at home in her bedroom with the door locked, inaccessible and unavailable. She left her room only to go to work or to dish out a random beating to one of us. Her mood and her room were dark at all times. She'd stick her head out from time to time to yell out orders for food and the stuff that mothers yell to children from their suicide bedrooms. When she hadn't stuck her head out for a while, I'd wonder if she was dead and stand with my ear pressed to her door, trying to pick up any sounds of life.

I feared her, and I knew I had to show it, because somehow it made her feel better about herself. But it wasn't just a show. I had a very real sense of unknowing, of expecting anything and everything to suddenly change for the worse at any minute. I was jittery all the time, and remained so well into adulthood.

Mom brought home a small bottle of powdered pink crystals one day, which sat on the side table in her bedroom. She warned us never to touch it, or we'd be harshly dealt with, which meant a yelling and a beating. It was poison, she told us, and if we continued to get on her nerves, she would kill herself. We grew to accept that if our mother ever committed suicide, we would be entirely responsible; it would be our punishment for being such wretched kids, for being alive. We lived in constant fear of that day. It was always imminent, an ever-present and steadily growing threat.

Meanwhile, our house continued to drown under the mess, clutter and general chaos. I spent days cleaning and tidying it up. Cleaning the house brought some kind of comfort and order; it fed my longing for beauty in the midst of this reign of sadness and fear.

I watched my mother's life wilt away, all the time feeling culpable for it. She hardly laughed, lost interest in her yummy cooking and handsome outfits, and in anything she'd ever considered beautiful or that once brought her joy. The only beautiful thing to my mother now was the bottle of pink poison.

One night as we were preparing for bed, Mom announced to me and my brother that tonight was the night she was going to kill herself. We would never lay our eyes on her again. It was 1990, the year our baby sister turned one. I was eleven.

She'd threatened suicide countless times before, so this wasn't anything new. But that night something in her words, in her tone of voice, was different, more determined. Terror rushed through me like an earthquake. I glanced over at my younger brother, and the fright in his hollow eyes bore into my soul. The choking helplessness I felt then still sends shudders through me. My utter despair at my inability to protect my siblings from the horror of our lives was completely overwhelming.

Her announcement made, she disappeared into her bedroom where the pink poison waited, and locked the door. Outside the door, we were left in deafening silence. Although my baby sister was asleep in the bedroom with Mom, in my mind she was right there with us, already motherless and abandoned to my care.

We did nothing, just huddled there together, the two of us, outside her bedroom door: Ahile's thin frame clinging to mine for comfort. For endless hours we huddled, not knowing what to expect. Would she open the door and give us hell, or was she already busy dying? I began to resign myself to a world without the only parent I had.

It was the longest night of my life, and it changed my life forever. That night all hope floated off into oblivion, disappearing like a hot-air balloon, drifting away until it was just a tiny, distant speck. I let go of love that night, and began to accept that life could still go on without it. I was undeserving, abandoned.

Halfway through the night we picked ourselves up off the floor and crawled numbly into bed, curled up half asleep in cold fear and anxiety. It didn't matter that our mother eventually emerged from her bedroom in the morning. I had already let go of her, together with the girl child Bonnie. Through that long night, all innocence slipped away, and my childhood came to an abrupt end.

6

Becoming

THE 74 BUS WAS THE BANE of my school days at Greenside High. Among that rowdy bunch of school kids I tried to be as invisible as possible. One afternoon during my first year there, I was at the bus stop as usual, trying to be inconspicuous to avoid getting noticed or mocked, when something unusual happened.

A pearly white, vintage-looking Mercedes-Benz pulled up at the bus stop. Out of it strutted a fiery redhead who began handing out small pamphlets. I was curious, but tried to look indifferent, although her enthusiasm and eccentric style weren't easy to ignore. Finally she made her way over to my end, greeted me with a smile and handed me a small pamphlet.

Do you want to be a TV STAR? it read.

I was shocked, not only by the sheer audacity of the words, but by the yearning it kindled inside me. I was embarrassed and confused. How could a nonentity like me – awkward, skinny and ugly as I was – even entertain such a thought? There were plenty of popular kids who would easily qualify for such a feat. Everything about me disqualified me; it was a no-brainer. This was a sick joke, and I wouldn't allow anyone the satisfaction of having me on. The vulnerability I felt in that moment was almost too much to bear.

As the woman strode back to her car, the bus stop erupted with shrieks and excited chatter at the possibility of stardom. It was the last day of term, so the atmosphere was particularly spirited. As the car pulled away, something seemed to catch the woman's attention, and she stopped again. Every eye was glued to her as she got out and made a beeline in my direction. I tried to step out of her way, but it became clear that it was me she was coming for. It would have been a good time for the earth to open up and swallow me whole. This was the sort of attention I made sure to avoid.

She stopped squarely in front of me, just inches away. Steadily engaging my gaze, she announced that I had a lovely face and that there was something special about me. Would I please be sure to come on Saturday morning for a screen test?

I thought I'd heard what she just said, and longed to wrap my stunted thoughts around it, but I really needed her to leave immediately, because there were now forty pairs of eyes on me, the number 74 had just arrived and my mind was in overdrive trying to think of a way to contain the damage she'd just done.

I slipped swiftly into the downstairs section of the

packed double decker, where no bullies usually sat. With the pamphlet safely scrunched in my blazer pocket, I tried to pretend that nothing had happened. The last thing I needed was to attract any more attention after the spectacle at the bus stop.

But no matter how I tried, I couldn't drown out the echo of her voice. Her words circled like bees in my mind, pollinating my heart with possibilities. I was in a daze. Had that really happened? Had someone seen something in me that wasn't in anybody else at the bus stop that day? Was I unique? Special? Did I really possess a presence and a beauty all my own?

That moment created a hunger in me, a hunger for more of those sweet words, words that called me out to take my place in the assembly line of purpose. Could I? The possibility overwhelmed and teased me. I would go for that screen test, not because I wanted to be on television, but because I needed to hear that affirmation again. To be told that I was special, significant; that there was good in me.

I told Mom about my encounter when she got home from work. She was busy at the kitchen sink as I tried to impress her with my story. Despite everything, my mother had never failed to express that she wanted the best for me, and had always thrust me into anything she believed would make my life turn out better than hers. She badly wanted me to escape the cycle of poverty and futility in the township around us, and would often despair at my lack of self-confidence. This, she decided, was an opportunity for me to outgrow the confines of my shell and draw me out. I saw no chance of that, but if it could earn me more affirming words, I was sold.

My mother called immediately to set up the screen test. I hadn't expected it to happen so fast, but on Saturday morning we found our way to Deirdre Smerczak's home office in Melville. I was extremely nervous, and wished my Mom wouldn't talk so much. She was prone to verbal diarrhoea when she got nervous, and would blurt out random and unnecessary information about me.

Deirdre explained that she would be putting me on camera. 'Call me Dee,' she said, leading us to the room where she shot her screen tests. She explained that it would be better if my mother waited in the chill room, to give me space to be free. As my mother turned to go, I saw the glint of hope in her eyes. Knowing that I had her full support was a huge reassurance.

'Be yourself,' Deirdre said. 'Be as relaxed and confident as possible, because the camera sees everything. It's like a mirror. Whatever's there, the camera's sure to pick up.' Surprisingly, I was completely okay with the idea; I didn't mind being peered at by a silent, inanimate entity. Dee pointed to a mark on the floor and asked me to restrict my movements so as not to move out of the camera frame.

She then focused the camera on me and asked me to look straight into the lens. I found the camera an unassuming and extremely comforting presence. It was unobtrusive, polite and non-judgemental – and best of all, it couldn't talk back. I locked my gaze on the lifeless black instrument and resolved to let it into places I'd never allowed any human to go. The only direction Dee gave was to introduce myself, to talk to the camera about myself and do whatever I wanted.

Amazingly, at the word 'Action', all my awkwardness melted away. As the camera came on, I came on, the world within me suddenly eager to express itself. Deep inside, something seemed to catch fire. I found a voice I'd never heard before. It had something to say, and it spoke with an undeniable certainty.

With the camera in my face I felt light; I was free, I was home. It was as if I'd finally come up for air after being under water all my life. And the camera accepted and absorbed everything I gave it, sucking it up like a sponge. It was a love dance.

That day, I didn't creep out of my shell, I leapt out like a Jack-in-the-box. Then, all too soon, the camera switched off, and Jack was back in the box. But Dee was beaming. Her hunch had paid off.

That Monday, Deirdre called my mom to say that a director had seen my screen test. He wanted me to audition for a thirteen-part mini-series called *Viva Families II*.

Mom rose to the occasion. She bent over backwards to get time off work to ferry me to the offices of the Professional Kids Agency, from where I got a lift with Dee. Since it was school holidays, the timing was perfect.

It all happened so fast. Everyone who saw my tape was thrilled. 'The camera loves you,' they told me. And soon I was juggling school, auditions and work.

Most of the work I got – commercials, presenting and a bit of acting – took place over weekends and school holidays. So when I wasn't at school, I was at work. I hardly saw my friends, but in some ways it was a relief not to be under pressure to socialise, because, quite frankly, I sucked at it.

Still, I'd sleep over some weekends at Katie's house in Northcliff, which I loved. In her household they all sat together as a family at mealtimes, chatting and laughing together, and because they were Scottish they'd eat haggis and dried ox blood. 'Try it, it's yummy,' Katie would say, but I wouldn't. Her parents were always interested in my life and my television work, and made me feel that they cared about my wellbeing. I fantasised about being adopted by them. 'Don't forget us when you're famous,' they'd say.

The entertainment industry was a foreign, grown-up world with very different rules, but for some reason I felt comfortable in it. I was a stranger there; I'd been given a clean slate. No one knew where I was from or that I was uncool at school; it was a brave new world, a chance to reinvent myself. The new me was a blend: a generous scoop of the old, a dab of what I saw the adults around me doing, and a smidgen of what I thought was expected of me.

For a thirteen-year-old, I made handsome money. *Viva Families II* paid R600 a call, and with around ten calls a month, I took home R6000 a month. I didn't care much about the money, but it felt good to be able to help out at home, and I happily handed it all over to my mother. It was the least I could do for all the grief she'd endured raising us. The extra income helped ease some of the pressure, although our expenses also seemed to increase, and Mom's mood didn't seem to lift. But now we never went to bed without supper again, and didn't always have to have sandwich spread on brown bread every day.

As hard as I tried to behave like an adult on set, my immaturity peeped out like a petticoat, giving away my age at unexpected moments. I often said the wrong thing at the wrong time, put my foot in it regularly and often needed help getting it out again from the very people I'd offended. I was just a mischievous kid, pulling pranks, joking around and trying to laugh and have fun even in the most serious situations. In a sense, it was the first chance I'd had to act my age. Back home I was too busy taking care of my mother, brother and sister, managing their tantrums, ironing their shirts, making their school lunches and cleaning house, and if I let any of these balls slip, I got a good hiding with a generous serving of insults. But this was the only life I knew, and many black kids lived under similar conditions or worse, because their parents, too, were wounded and broken under the violence visited upon them by apartheid. The only way to wade through the decay that had become the black family unit was to keep moving, keep your head up and not give in to tears. '*Ukukhala akusizi*. Crying doesn't help.'

7

First Love

IN STANDARD EIGHT I FELL in love with a boy I met while shooting a television ad. The narrative was a cute story in which the life and soul of a party eyed the wallflower, and finally followed her to the kitchen as she fetched a platter of food for the guests. It was instant attraction and the ad ended just as their lips were about to touch. In a case of life imitating art, my co-actor, the handsome, confident Clenton, got hold of my number and called me the next day.

Clenton Motaung was a presenter on the popular kids' channel, KTV. He was three years older than me, cool, charismatic and smooth, and drew attention wherever he went, especially from girls. My stomach did a butterfly disco when he asked me to the movies after a chat.

We could never spend as much time together as we wanted, what with us both juggling school and work. He soon took me home to meet his parents, but I never really knew how they felt about me. Although I got on well with his guy friends, the girls in his crowd didn't welcome me.

Clenton was such a gentleman, sweet and sincere, always speaking softly and kindly to me. He charmed my mother with his politeness, brought me home at the agreed time and never pushed me to do anything I wasn't ready for. To my delight, he asked me to his matric dance, to which I wore a long, tight black dress. My mom helped me shop for it, and I still remember the look in his eyes when he picked me up; he couldn't stop telling me how beautiful I looked.

Although I loved him dearly, I wasn't ready for a sexual relationship, and after turning him down a few times, I started to fear he'd leave me for a girl who was ready. When he finished school, he became co-host on the *Top Forty* show on Radio 5, and things got really exciting for him.

We dated for a year, during which I grew familiar with love's dips and turns. Then one Saturday morning I picked up the newspaper and learnt that he was dead. He and his best friend had been in a horrific car accident the previous evening.

The bottom fell out of my world. Mom wept with me that day, jerked back to her own pain of losing my father. Gutted, I felt as though life had spitefully snatched my title deed to happiness right out of my hand. The funeral and memorial service were filled with colleagues and students all mourning the loss of someone so special, and it brought me and his friends closer; our differences seemed insignificant now in the face of our loss.

Clenton's death threw my whole world into disarray, and the emptiness remained for a long time afterwards. I'd try to study for exams, but the words on the pages made no sense. I became a ghost, floating like a stranger through school and home, wishing I'd died with him. One day I broke down in school and had to be sent home. Yet, in spite of the gaping hole I was catapulted into, Clenton had awakened both the knowledge that it was possible for me to be someone's beloved and my longing for love. In the end, this longing began to supersede the pain, and I managed to recover and continue dreaming of possibilities, of beautiful things to come. And it felt good.

I still lived in my imagination. I could disconnect and be transported effortlessly to new worlds. I became addicted to the detachment I found in the chasm between the real and the imagined. But I never dared to look down, because I sensed that beneath lurked a black river of insanity that threatened to sweep me off my feet. Anxiety remained my loyal companion, and my survival depended on staying in control. Control was like a delicately tensioned thread that I used to support my will to live. But it wasn't easy to maintain. Brooding just under the surface was a great pressure that threatened to rise up and engulf me, to carry me away on a wave of madness. Sometimes it disguised itself as a premonition of disaster, a pending calamity that could overtake me at any time. But the trick was in the control.

My anxiety would catch me laughing and remind me that the sweetness was fleeting. Maybe I'd learnt the habit as a child. When Mom saw me having fun she'd say, 'You're too happy, watch out. Tears are around the corner.' If I felt a hint of warmth and belonging, fear reminded me that it couldn't be. I dared not let down my guard; I had to keep control. I kept joy and frivolity at arm's length; I couldn't afford to grow attached in case it deserted me.

People who looked at me saw it differently. They saw aloofness, a distant, grudging gaze. 'You look bored,' they'd say, 'You look high,' or more often, 'You look like you don't want to be here.' Little did they know how afraid I was of them, and afraid of being there. I was scared of pretty much everything: scared of people, scared of their emotions, and scared of my own. So I suppressed anything I didn't know what to do with. It was safer that way.

'I'm okay, just tired,' I'd say.

Meanwhile, life at home became more and more unbearable. My mother continued to beat us senseless in her relentless fits of rage. Every act or omission was punishable and the punishment was unrelated to the seriousness of the offence. I found a way to suppress every feeling, holding my breath till the beating was over. I found I could drown out the pain if I stretched my torso over my knees, with eyes squeezed shut, my face buried between my thighs and stomach. As the pain charged through me like electricity, I'd surf to my imagined paradise on the flashes of lightning each blow brought.

Nothing good I did mattered, and I'd long since given up trying to earn praise. There was no point in doing well at school, and it didn't matter if I slept with boys; I was already a whore in my mother's eyes anyway. I'd even overheard my mother telling her friend that I was a whore. I grew sure that something more was wrong with me than just having stolen my mom's dreams.

Even though she stopped beating me when I turned fifteen, I still couldn't stop her torrent of cruel words; her verbal abuse tore through me like a hot knife. And I watched her become increasingly violent with my brother. She once hurled a rock at him and opened a deep gash in his head. Blinded by tears, I tried desperately to staunch the bleeding, while he howled and my mother went right on hurling insults at him.

I made many a plan to run away, but always discarded the idea out of fear that she'd find me and beat me, and fear of leaving my siblings to face the terror alone. There wasn't much I could do to protect them, but I hoped my presence was at least a show of support and solidarity.

8

Deeper

WHEN MY SIX-WEEK STINT with *Viva Families II* ended, I landed a gig hosting a show on a TV learning series called *Teleschool*. Soon after that, I moved on to present a funky weekly magazine programme called *ZapMag* on TV1. My co-hosts were two vibrant young boys, one of whom was Vusi Twala.

I didn't like Vusi at all at first. His self-satisfied confidence offended me as much as it intrigued me, and I was careful to keep my defences up at all costs. I never missed an opportunity to show my disapproval or voice a different opinion. He and Gill, the other presenter, were as thick as thieves, and enjoyed making fun of me. They teased me about my boyfriend who did kiddy shows. But I suspected that they actually envied him, because they seemed to be rather too interested in who I was dating.

The news of Clenton's death caught everyone off guard, and I was touched by the beautiful bouquet of flowers and condolences from Vusi and Gill. They also seemed to feel guilty for their teasing about him in light of the unfortunate turn of events. I began to see a softer, more sensitive side to Vusi, who became kinder and gentler with me after that.

As we worked together we became friends. He was different from the boys I'd met before; he had a dream that glittered so brightly it made my eyes water. He carried a rare, fresh perspective on life, thrusting out from the realm of dullness, daring me to come to the cliff's edge to engage with what lay beneath. He was a child star just like me, and we helped each other get a grip on a reality few people our age were experiencing. He had an awkwardness about him too, and around him my own awkwardness found a place to rest and be accepted. His own detachment and aloofness drew me to him, and we found solace in each other's strangeness. He made me laugh; he had a way with words that intoxicated me. We circled and fluttered around each other for months in the studio, on set, in the make-up room and in the corridors. Each time we spoke, our souls whispered invitations to each other, and we began to fall in love in the gentlest, most unobtrusive way. By the time we finally held hands, we found we'd already travelled many roads together.

After a couple of months we were swept off our feet by a passionate romance that the wildest waters couldn't quench. We became inseparable. We understood each other's worlds and most things didn't have to be explained. At times words even became too much, for we feared they would strain the tenderness between us. We had so many things in common, especially the fact that we didn't do what other teenagers did on weekends.

My time at work brought me some much-needed relief. It was the only time I got to let go and dream, to feel like a normal teenage girl, even if only for a few hours. Our dance gradually unfolded within the safe environment of long, lazy lunches with his family, adrenalin-filled shooting schedules and silent tears cupped in each other's hands. Vusi supported me emotionally as best he could; he offered a shoulder to cry on and a space where I could let out my pain. And our relationship brought me many rich gifts that fed my soul.

Vusi Twala became my hero. To me he was the prototype of maleness, the original stencil. With him my life made sense and took shape. For a year it was pure friendship, and we'd fall asleep peacefully in each other's arms, feeling no pressure to indulge in anything more. When we crossed the line into the deeper waters of intimacy it was a natural progression, a safe place where I learnt about my body as he studied it. I discovered my own sensuality, and the intoxicating charm of a strong arm nestling in the small of my back.

On the weekends when we weren't shooting *ZapMag*, I spent a lot of time with him and his colourful family. It was a welcome escape from the heavy load at home. They were wonderful to me and teased me lovingly. I had peroxided my hair, and Vusi's uncle, Sandile, nicknamed me Rodman, after the basketball player who'd also bleached his hair.

Vusi's mother, the iconic Shado Twala, enthralled me. She was a radio broadcaster and media mogul, well known for her enchanting, sultry voice and her love and knowledge of jazz. Ironically, my mom told me that while she was dating my father and they were madly in love, my father never missed Shado's radio show because he couldn't get enough of her voice.

I'd never encountered anyone like Shado. Despite her petite body, she was a strong-willed woman with a formidable personality and a laugh that came right from the bottom of her belly. She embraced me, took me in, and welcomed me into the sisterhood of life, affirming my femininity. I loved her and always wanted to be around her. To me she was a rare kind of interesting, and she epitomised freedom and individuality. Conversations with her revealed a kaleidoscope of ideas. She had a sophisticated and stylish wardrobe, a home filled with memorabilia, pictures and trinkets from her many travels, and she cooked the most delectable food.

She also had an incredible music collection, and greatly influenced my taste in music. Weekends spent at their home were one continuous music lesson, a soul encounter with good food, music, conversation and acceptance. Now, when I was at home, I'd spend hours compiling taped music off the radio on my cassette player. I could listen to music endlessly, floating between the lines, winding my emotions around the strings of melody, soothed by the knowledge that somewhere, someone else had known the loneliness I knew, and had lived to sing about it.

Music became a healing balm caressing my wounds, numbing the pain. As I taped songs from Radio Metro, I fell in love with the likes of Anita Baker, Nina Simone, Dionne Warwick, Aretha Franklin and Tracy Chapman. They spoke my pain, romanticising my melancholy with their words. In their artistry I found a balm to patch my heart back together again, in the hope that maybe I could bear up, carry on and perhaps even thrive. The magic of music enchanted my soul, silencing the deep pressure – if only fleetingly.

Vusi became a monument in my life, and his family became my own. When he spoke, he showed me the world, painting pictures of possibilities I'd only read about in books, energising me with his appetite for life. The atmosphere between us was pure, undiluted passion. But it was almost dangerous at times. For by then I'd perfected the art of travelling with my mind to inhabit worlds I'd never set foot in, and so I projected myself completely into Vusi's world. I never communicated in any detail to him what was going on in my home life. Instead, I enjoyed the escape from my world, and didn't want to dampen the atmosphere between us with the heaviness of my problems at home. I kept my different worlds apart. I lived through him when my own life was too cluttered. I lived in his world and wanted nothing else but to believe in and carry his dream. I was also willing to let go of my own secret imagined wonderland in favour of this new world of his, which was bigger, more glamorous and more perfect.

We never discussed marriage, but we'd page through magazines together choosing furniture for our future home. Being apart wasn't something we could imagine. But we were young and our lives were changing, and every change affected the balance between us.

Soon after I finished school, *ZapMag* came to an end, and I became co-presenter on the new show that replaced it, *Limits Unlimited*. But Vusi and Gill were no longer hosts – they became the directors, and started their own production company, Jewazi (a collaboration between a Jew and a Swazi). Vusi became really busy now, and spent all his time with Gill, even though I was involved in the same show. It left me feeling neglected and unappreciated. When he bought his first car, a red BMW, I wasn't included in the big event.

At the beginning of the following year, under pressure

from my mother, I enrolled at Wits Technikon to study Public Relations, and moved into the students' residence. Conveniently, the campus was a stone's throw from the SABC where the TV show was recorded, so I could just bounce back and forth like a ping pong ball.

I attended classes most days, but I hated it. My face was well known now, so students recognised me and ogled shamelessly no matter what I did. They never really got comfortable having me there, and would do anything to get my attention. I took to sitting at the back of the class during lectures to avoid attracting attention to myself, and constantly wore sunglasses. I became a total recluse. I was lonely, and never felt like I connected with anyone because they couldn't relax and treat me normally – they always seemed to have an ulterior motive for being with me. So I started bunking lectures and hanging out in the cafeteria eating hot chips – the best I'd ever tasted – with lashings of watery tomato sauce. I'd follow this with two or three cigarettes, and then stare blankly into the distance wondering how to fill the emptiness inside me.

After three months of trying to act like a normal student, I woke up one morning and decided never to go back. I didn't feel I owed anyone an explanation, since I was the one paying for it anyway. Mom was extremely disappointed, and always eager to let me know. But by now I'd given up caring or trying to please her. I'd spent enough time trying to win her approval without success, so I knew I was damned anyway. My relationship with Vusi was faltering at this stage; I wasn't seeing that much of him, and I missed him and his family badly.

I moved out of the students' residence at the same time, and found a place in Lyndhurst in a complex called Le Cascine.

When *Limits Unlimited* came to an end shortly afterwards, I became extremely anxious. For the first time I was on my own with rent to pay. Fortunately, Vusi made a couple of calls on my behalf and organised me an audition for the show *Technics Heart of the Beat*. A couple of days later, I had the job.

9

Losing My Religion

WHEN I MOVED OUT of my mother's home in Soweto, I packed up my awkwardness along with my belongings. But I was determined to shake it loose.

Out of home and in the land of the free, my life took a drastic turn. I took to smoking and drinking – habits I thoroughly enjoyed – and to late-night partying at Tandoor in Yeoville. I also stopped going to church. I still didn't get the point of church, and every now and then I'd cast a what-have-you-done-for-me-lately glance towards heaven.

On Sunday mornings, Mom would call. 'Beware, Bonnie, I know you're drinking and smoking. God's going to punish you.' I believed he would, but I was beyond caring. In fact, I was daring him. I mean, how much worse could it get? My whole life had felt like one long punishment.

Vusi and I began to fight increasingly and mistrust each other's intentions, and before long we'd changed so much that we no longer recognise each other. My newfound independence made Vusi uncomfortable, as though I'd crossed into a space he couldn't control or define. When he found a pack of cigarettes in my room one day it sparked a huge fight, and he insisted I flush it down the toilet and never do it again.

It didn't help that my mom would randomly call Vusi to tell him what a terrible daughter I was, which left him feeling that there was a side to me he didn't know and caused a lot of mistrust. I felt she was deliberately ruining any chance I had at happiness, reminding me that I didn't deserve it. Though we still loved each other, amid the growing noise of publicity, money and career pressure, we could no longer tune into each other's heart channels and share the pain and new challenges that came at us. Like the end of a movie, our relationship was slowly fading to black.

I was losing not just the love of my life but his whole family, without the chance to even explain it to them. They were watching it playing out right in front of them but without the audio to go with it.

After five years, our relationship finally buckled under the pressure of our brokenness. But we struggled to let each other go. The next four years were punctuated by painful midnight rendezvous in between our other relationships, which could never match what we'd had together. We were both hurting, dealing with issues in ways we couldn't articulate. Both having grown up on television, ours was a strange reality, so much so that at times I felt ill-equipped to function socially, let alone have a normal relationship. I was twenty-four before we were finally able to close the door on this tumultuous emotional roller coaster.

Our break-up frayed the cords of my heart, leaving me even more damaged than when our relationship began. I convinced myself that if Vusi couldn't love me, no one could. If he no longer saw me, I'd disappear. In my mind, I was because Vusi was. It took time to scrub him out of my soul; the connection was so strong, it threatened the survival of any other relationship, and I had to fight very hard to untangle myself from its grip. I'd met him at a time when I needed and ached for a reason to live, to hold on and believe again.

My neediness had placed a heavy weight on us, and laid too much expectation on him and the relationship; I'd made it the answer to everything and worshipped at its altar. I hated my world and wanted to escape forever into the one we'd created together. I didn't understand at that time that a healthy relationship needed two healthy, growing people, not refugees. So, inevitably, I got burnt. All the suppressed emotion I'd kept bottled up inside began to seep through the strained stitches of my patchwork soul. And now that I'd broken up with Vusi, it was as though a toxic sweat was breaking on the surface of my skin, burning it away like acid.

One day, in a wild demonstration of my newfound freedom, I popped down to Rockey Street to get myself a tattoo on my back. When the tattoo artist asked which design I wanted, I looked at all the patterns plastered around his studio walls, and chose the most mysterious and abstract of the lot, without bothering to find out if it meant anything – who cared, anyway? That same week I got a tongue ring, and a few weeks later a belly ring. My hairstyle fluctuated between peroxide blonde and completely bald. Finally I was breaking out of my shell of isolation; I was determined to become a child of the world, one the world could call its own.

I was living life on my own terms now, and I lived extravagantly without a thought – and without sparing a cent. I relished being irresponsible and not having to take care of anybody but myself. I was determined to make up for all the time that I'd been forced to behave like an adult, carrying responsibilities way beyond my means to handle. Now I could stay up as late as I wanted, leave my flat unkempt and let dishes pile up for days.

Beneath this life makeover brewed a hungry rage: anger at my mother, at the world and at God. Years of repression had taken their toll – years of being treated as a huge disappointment and blamed for making my mother's life a living hell – and now anger raged in my chest like a fire-breathing dragon. My awkwardness and my anger had become bedfellows while I wasn't looking, and I had no idea how to control this world inside me, which felt so crowded.

The slightest provocation triggered unwarranted eruptions of anger, and with each eruption, the monkey on my back grew heavier. These blow-ups took place at work, with friends and even with fans. I became labelled as aloof and cold, which I didn't altogether mind as long as people kept their distance. It meant they were less likely to hurt me. I was so afraid of being hurt or rejected, I would avoid anything that hinted at the possibility. It wasn't that I was deliberately putting on a look, but it seemed that way to others. And I grew to accept it.

My on-screen presence on *Technics Heart of the Beat* drew much curiosity from the public and the media, and my bored-to-death look went everywhere with me. With my growing presence in the entertainment industry came countless invitations to parties, events, launches and award ceremonies. I always rose to the occasion and dressed to the nines, attitude and all. Whenever I was in a room, people couldn't keep their eyes off me. I had become a phenomenon, a strange and mysterious breed of woman, but their intrigue was tempered with caution because the look on my face said *'ungangijwayeli kabi'* (don't get too familiar); I bite.

The power and attention were intoxicating. But at times they were completely intrusive, and left me feeling completely exposed. I feared that intuitive individuals could pick up my awkwardness and insecurity, my sense of not belonging, the way locals spot a foreigner from a mile away. What country was I from, then, anyway? Where were my people, and would I ever find them? These questions reverberated endlessly through my mind, echoing a deep loneliness, a void that no amount of praise and attention could fill. I felt like a misfit, always on the fringes looking in. Everywhere I went I was surrounded by people – loving friends and adoring fans, and yet loneliness stuck like a film to my skin; loneliness *was* me.

I didn't mind fans at a distance, but they got under my skin at times. Someone always seemed to ask the most inappropriate question or make a demeaning remark. 'You're way shorter than I thought you'd be.' 'Have you gained weight?' This tendency was more prevalent among black people, who seemed completely comfortable saying things only the closest of friends and family should be allowed to say; they took unearned privileges to voice whatever they liked within minutes of meeting me. This pressed my buttons and annoyed me more than it should have. When I vented this frustration among friends, they'd say, 'You're public property now. It comes with the territory.' But their words only fuelled my defiance at being owned or forced to conform to any code imposed on me by random members of the public.

My close friendship with Thandiswa Mazwai at this time helped to give meaning to those empty, lonely spaces that came with fame. With her I felt safe, seen and understood. We really got each other. We'd met at the complex in

Lyndhurst where I lived, where she often popped in to see another friend. After a mutual friend introduced us, she dropped in to say hello, and found me listening to Skunk Anansie. We connected like superglue, and listened to Skunk Anansie together for many moons. Soon we were doing everything together. I loved her defiant, resilient spirit, her remarkable talent and uncommon way of expressing herself. We connected like sisters and our friendship lasted many years.

We guarded our space fiercely, helping each other weather the rough seas of fame and fortune. But trouble followed me: I still felt like a misfit with a constant urge to rebel against the status quo. My mother's disapproving eyes seemed to lurk in the most unexpected places, as if they'd taken on a personality of their own, and I'd spot them out the corner of my eye whenever I'd found a place to just be. They were my invisible prison warder, always watching to make sure I never escaped. Maybe I was the one holding on to them, as if they were tattooed onto my identity. I felt like I was nothing without them, and yet there was always the faint possibility that I could be everything without them.

My life was steeped in drama. Chaos followed me, brewing anxiety in its stormy waters, and although the drama was draining, it also gave me an adrenalin fix, a high I could ride until the next wave. Drama became addictive, albeit exhausting.

I developed an unquenchable shopping addiction and its appetite grew more ravenous with every purchase. It was no respecter of persons, responsibilities or bills; my finances became a Hiroshima of debt, late rental payments and impulsive spending. I didn't care. I had accounts at Edgars, Truworths and Woolworths, which I paid only when I felt like it, and a Standard Bank overdraft that was growing at an alarming rate. I had to keep up the fast and easy lifestyle I felt the industry demanded of me, and I was more than happy to oblige.

The chaos on the outside was symbolic of how I felt inside. It reflected the true state of my soul, and it was only bearable because I didn't care; I was completely indifferent. The anger dragon had pumped me up into a state of rebellion that knew no limits; it gave me the kind of high I imagine a heroin user might feel right after shooting up. Moments of clarity were an unwelcome intrusion, and to deal with the chaos my life had become, I simply created more chaos.

10

Walkabout

I ENJOYED ARRIVING AT WORK as my plain ordinary self, sitting through an hour or so of make-up and wardrobe and emerging transformed, like Cinderella at the ball. It was every girl's dream, and at nineteen years old, I had it as my job. My co-presenter, Glen Lewis, was well known for his deejaying and house music, as well as for the show he hosted on Metro FM. He was like an older brother: funny, kind and helpful, and always ready to lend a hand and give advice. Glen taught me a lot about music, and our show grew very popular.

But shooting *Technics Heart of the Beat* took up only half a day every second week, and even with industry appearances and interviews, I had plenty of free time. It left me restless and on the prowl for a new challenge.

Through industry functions I met Christina Storm, a dynamic young model making serious waves in the industry, and I was greatly impressed by her nonchalance and her flawless beauty. She was convinced I could carve out a successful modelling career for myself, and suggested I join the modelling agency that represented her. So, on her advice, I went along to see Leanna at Next Models. Leanna was a feisty woman with a deep, resonant voice, and we took an immediate liking to each other.

The modelling scene was unapologetically all about appearance. I was used to this from my television work, but the modelling world took the obsession with perfection to another level. Your contribution hinged on your appearance alone, and I was shocked at people's candour about what they thought of your looks. At that time I had mild acne, and discussions about it went on right in front of me, without including me. I had to grow crocodile skin not to end up in tears.

I was required to compile a portfolio – a collection of photos of myself in a variety of outfits, including a face shot, a body shot, and so on. I had to supply my own selection of clothes and pay a photographer and a make-up artist, which would set me back about R1200, a lot of money in 1999. I found the whole process nerve-wracking. When my test shoot was done, the pictures were slotted into plastic sleeves in a funky metal folder with the word NEXT embossed on the front.

With my portfolio in hand, I began to attend go-sees with beauty and fashion editors at magazines, ad agencies and department stores. Some of these were just plain castings, mockingly referred to as cattle calls, at which up to a thousand models might audition for a single role, usually in an ad. With a number pinned to my chest, I'd walk into the room and parade before the menacing decision-makers, waiting for the disappointed puppet eyes and a grimacing suck of air through the teeth.

'Turn around. Profile left! Profile right! Take off your clothes!' The agencies always warned us to wear a bikini beneath our clothes in case the casting director needed to see our bodies. 'Turn around! Thank you! *Next!*'

Throughout those barked instructions, any awkwardness, any insecurity about your stretch marks or the size of your behind had to be neatly tucked away, because the slightest whiff of uncertainty sent the panel of poker faces gunning for you like wolves at the scent of blood. The more confidence you faked, the less chance you'd be picked on.

Some in the industry were especially known for their rude and malicious comments, and I had sleepless nights at the thought of these dreaded encounters. Every model knew they had to wear their thickest skins to the cattle calls, and castings for Fashion Week were my worst.

On my first ever go-see with the then beauty editor of *Elle* magazine, Dawn Mpathi, I took great pains to look my best. Despite the tight knot in my stomach and my lack of confidence about my acne-prone skin, I took the forty-kilometre trip into town by taxi to meet her. I didn't expect her to be the friendliest of people; after all, she carried the heavy load of being a black woman working for the oh-so-prestigious *Elle* magazine. But that day goes down in history as the worst of my modelling experience. Dawn gave me her famous up, down and around in just eight seconds, and then flipped through my portfolio with disdain.

'This,' (meaning me) 'is absolutely unacceptable!' she pronounced. She then proceeded to describe in detail why nothing about me represented the calibre of model *Elle* used. 'Appalling,' she concluded.

It was like something out of an American chick flick, glorifying the level of malice that women in the fashion and beauty industry have been known to visit upon each other. I'm not certain how I managed to get from her office to the taxi rank without falling apart. Peeling myself off the floor on which she'd trampled me took quite a bit of doing. Echoing through my brain all the while was, 'What the hell were you thinking?' I eventually made my way home and collapsed on my bed in tears. She was fully within her rights to deny me the job, but the contempt with which she'd treated me felt unnecessary and undeserved, because I just didn't know better. It wasn't my fault my skin was acne prone, and at that point I didn't have the means to fix it.

As hurt as I'd been by that meeting, I decided in my heart to make her eat her words. I kept on doing go-sees and castings – in between the glamorous partying and drinking that went with the modelling lifestyle – and I began getting modelling jobs. One of my first was a fashion spread for *True Love* magazine, for which we travelled to the Cape Verde islands. As excited as I was at the adventure, I ended up loathing every minute of it. My reserved manner caused offence. It felt to me as if there was an unwritten code that models should constantly suck up to their fashion editors and make-up artists, make mindless small talk and shower them with false compliments, as if grovelling in gratitude for having been chosen among many hopefuls. I didn't subscribe to the code, and was soon labelled difficult to work with. On our return, the magazine editor called to tell me that her magazine wouldn't hire me again. It was a one-way conversation, with no attempt to let me speak. I felt that my crime was that I hadn't worn a constant smile and stroked the fashion editor's ego.

Nevertheless, I got other fashion shoots doing catalogues for Jet and Woolworths, and also a few ads and beauty shoots.

Summer was modelling season. Models from all over the country and abroad would travel to Cape Town and stay in communes called model houses, which were a crazy melting pot of hot chicks, big egos and cat fights. I spent one season in Cape Town and scored a few jobs, one of which was an underwear catalogue for Woolworths, which remains one of my favourite shoots. The photographers and editors in Cape Town seemed more relaxed than those in Jo'burg, and we could easily walk from one casting to the next, spend the afternoon on the beach and then cruise over to Long Street for a drink. If a place was a bit too far to walk, we caught little open-door taxis called Rikkis that zipped through the traffic at lightning speed, all for a mere five rand.

So I persevered, got my foot in the door and soon became successful as a model. I even got rated among the most talked-about black faces. This was the era when the Face of Africa was born, and the fashion and beauty industry used us as a canvas on which to explore the essence of black beauty. And within a year of my first go-see with Dawn Mpathi, *Elle* magazine used me on a number of wonderful fashion and beauty shoots, which remain some of the gems in my portfolio.

But the modelling industry was cutthroat, and there were bound to be incidents that could break your spirit. In 2000 *Cosmopolitan* magazine hired me for an advertorial for a handbag brand. The fashion editor at the time was a lovely lady who loved my look and enjoyed pushing the boundaries in her shoots. We did a beautiful shoot and I was looking forward to its appearance in *Cosmo*, but at higher levels it was decided that the readership wouldn't identify with a black girl, so they reshot it with a white model. It hurt to know that the colour of my skin was ultimately more important than beauty, talent or individuality, and it forever altered my view of *Cosmopolitan*.

But within two years of joining Next Models, my path was increasingly pointing towards acting. Although I was now successful as a model, I was bored. I felt I couldn't go on being the pretty smiling face or the thin-enough body to sell whatever whoever wanted to sell. It just wasn't enough – I had more to give. Ever since my first acting experience at *Viva Families II*, the idea of telling stories had struck a chord with me and I secretly longed for that experience again. I would watch the likes of Judi Dench, Anthony Hopkins, Denzel Washington or Robert De Niro, study their manner, gestures and character interpretations, and be transfixed by the magic they seemed to produce so effortlessly. This was what I longed to do. I wanted to speak, to work with ideas, to reveal a beauty deeper than make-up and the latest fashion.

So I gave up modelling for good. But it had certainly played its part in paying my bills, increasing my influence and moulding my confidence, and all those shut doors and menacing faces I'd come up against had helped thicken my skin for the still-generous amounts of rejection that come with acting.

11

Fame

TECHNICS HEART OF THE BEAT was fast gaining popularity. Presenting involved a direct conversation with the audience, and I really enjoyed it. Whereas acting involved assuming someone else's personality, presenting allowed me to be myself and showcase my personality while making things fun and interesting for the viewer. My light banter with co-host Glen Lewis became a highlight, and I became known for my quirky, laid-back style.

We played a wide spectrum of music genres and appealed to all kinds of music tastes. We also got to interview many local and international musicians, and because I had more free time than Glen, I did most of the interviews. Among them were iconic musicians such as Bheki Mseleku, Abbey

Lincoln, Sibongile Khumalo, Luther Vandross, Jonathan Butler and Janet Jackson. I remember Janet admiring my shoes and asking where she could get a pair. Other icons we interviewed included Lynden David Hall, Ringo Madlingozi, Busi Mhlongo, Youssou N'Dour and the brothers K-Ci and JoJo Hailey. JoJo, in an attempt to seduce me, told me that he and Mary J Blige were over. But I would be dumb, I decided, to pick up what she had cast off, so it wasn't such a great pick-up line after all.

This was a time in our country when young black artists were starting to spread their wings and express themselves through music, poetry and dance. Kwaito was beginning to thrive, moulding the voice of a generation, providing an outlet for everything it had ever suppressed or just wanted to say, and it had an attentive audience. The party culture was in vogue, with six-to-six bashes and the likes of TKZee burning up the dance floors. Kwaito music gave this culture a voice, doing for young black South African identity what hip hop had done for American youth. Boom Shaka was tearing up stages around the country with Lebo Mathosa emerging as the femme fatale, taking what Brenda Fassie had done to the next level. Meanwhile, Thandiswa Mazwai was giving a voice to the more conscious thinkers, telling the truth about where we were at as a people and a nation, taking it to a more spiritual space.

And there I was, from the age of nineteen, meeting all these incredible musicians from across the globe, and getting the chance to sit and converse with them. *Technics Heart of the Beat* placed me at the very centre of all this activity. I was the face of the music culture; I got to hang out with the best of the best, and they all wanted to impress me. With my tattoo, bald head, outspoken manner and ice-queen demeanour, I represented the new generation of black women. We had something to say and refused to be dismissed as just pretty faces. And yet, wrapped in a thick fog of sadness and anxiety, I failed to fully notice or celebrate the significance of it all. And maybe in a way that was also a good thing, because at least it kept me calm.

I'd been on television for five years already, but now I had a prime-time slot and captured a larger, older audience. People who'd never heard the name Bonnie Mbuli heard it on this show. Everybody, it seemed, wanted a piece of me now. They wanted to know what rare planet I'd come from. I was a pioneer, a trendsetter. Girls wanted to be me; boys and men promised me heaven and earth. I was the youngest black woman hosting a music television show of that magnitude at that time in South Africa, and my look, approach and manner set the benchmark for what was to follow in South Africa, and blazed a trail for many young people in television.

I was a ground breaker, just like my mother – her ceiling had become my floor. Yet I couldn't quite enjoy or grasp the magnitude of all I had access to. I lacked the presence of mind or soul to realise or capitalise on the legacy I was building. No amount of hype and excitement around my name could soothe my pain or gain the approval or applause of the one person from whom I needed it most. Watching myself on television every Tuesday night was indescribably difficult; I was intensely self-critical and noticed every last tiny imperfection. I also felt very removed from the Bonnie I watched on television. I couldn't quite relate to her; she seemed so different from me.

Now everything I did made news. The media scrutiny overwhelmed me, and I wore sunglasses wherever I went. My ice-queen look said, 'Stay away; don't step up to ask dumb questions. I'm not in the mood.' While the hype did swell my head in one sense, and I clung to it as some kind of compensation for all my childhood heartache, ironically, my anxiety and self-doubt helped to keep me close to the ground, humbling and earthing me like a heavy rope around my waist, a harness to stop me falling over the edge.

With time on my hands, I decided to get a job as a waitress. By now I had an innate desire to get back to basics; I wanted normality, routine. My life had become too contrived and lofty for my own liking, and I longed to be an ordinary girl in her twenties, battling it out at the same level as every other young adult. Waitressing wasn't about the money, but reflected a desire to connect with normal people who weren't the fabulous industry folk; people I could have real conversations with, who had ordinary problems and lives. I'd been on television and in the spotlight since I was thirteen, and now in my early twenties I craved to experience another world. It was partly the rebel in me, the anti-celebrity. So I got myself a job at The House of Coffees in Melville, on the corner of Fourth Avenue and Seventh Street, not far from home.

It was awkward, to say the least. Customers – mostly black ones – would recognise me and ask why I was waitressing. There wasn't much to say, except that I wanted to. My colleagues found my story quite amusing, always asking questions and trying to understand why on earth I was doing it if I didn't have to. Mostly I enjoyed the intrigue and the curiosity garnered by my story. But some days I'd just show up at work with a book, give all my tables away to colleagues and sit reading, pretending to work whenever Lawrence, the manager, showed up. Like any normal waitress, I was sometimes treated rudely by customers, and was occasionally rude back. It was amusing to watch people with a sense of importance treat me as the lowest of the low because I was just a measly waitress – knowing nothing of my real story. I accepted it as part of the whole experience, but if they took it too far I put my foot down.

Lawrence was always super nice to me, and didn't deal as harshly with me as with other waiters; he seemed to take my other job into consideration. I made many interesting friends in the waitressing scene, and after work we'd all go and knock back shooters at Question Mark, the restaurant next door. But eventually, after I'd waitressed for a year, my real work got too busy and I had to quit.

12

Bad Girl

I was hanging out with Thandiswa in Melville one afternoon when we spotted a For Sale sign on a white convertible Beetle with a red leather interior. 'It's hot, my friend. *Iyarocka!* It rocks!' squealed Thandiswa. 'I'd get it if I were you.'

I was smitten. I called the number, and two days later it was mine. I'd paid R25 000 cash, and all that was left to do was to change its ownership at the traffic department and drive it home. Here was the biggest problem: I couldn't drive. So I called up my friend, Thomas Msengana, aka Bad Boy T, and asked him to drive it home for me.

On the way home he kept asking me questions. 'Did you get the tyres checked? Did you take it to a garage to get it checked over?' I hadn't, of course. All I knew was that it was time I got a car, so I had. What counted was that I'd done it *my* way.

Thomas left the car in my designated parking bay in the complex I'd recently moved to in Auckland Park. Each day after that I walked past it on my way to catch a bus, a metered taxi or a lift with a friend. And each time I wondered when I'd actually learn to drive and get my licence. And my frustration grew.

After about a week I decided that I'd watched enough people drive and there was a simple pattern to it. With all the questions I'd asked Thomas on our drive home, I'd also picked up a thing or two, and I could figure out the rest along the way. I was good to go. So I got into the car and drove.

My first trip was a thirty-five-kilometre drive to Thandiswa's place in Morningside during peak traffic. Wearing my big shades and a look of defiance, I drove in first gear all the way. Although I had no clue what I was doing, come hell or high water, I was going to teach myself to drive. And that's exactly what I did. I knocked the occasional pole, rubbish bin and tow bar of another car, but a month after that first painstaking drive to Morningside, I could drive.

The more familiar I became with my bombshell of a car, the more I realised just how much was wrong with it. I was furious at the seller's dishonesty, but I knew it served me right for not doing the whole thing properly like sensible people do. I could so easily have asked the Automobile Association to check the car before I bought it. But I wasn't going to cry over spilt milk, even if I was now stuck with a car that broke down regularly. And because I'd refused to pay someone to teach me how to drive, let alone got a licence before buying it, I'd managed to turn my car into a *skorokoro* (wreck) in a matter of weeks, which caused me much embarrassment.

The manual soft top was of hardly any use as the fittings were irregular, and the windows didn't fit snugly into the top when it was on, which meant I got drenched when it rained.

On the night of the Lenny Kravitz concert at Ellis Park, I was in Yeoville in the early evening and hit heavy traffic on the way to the concert. I found myself slap bang in the middle of a bumper-to-bumper bottleneck, looking ever so cool in my convertible and my matching puffy red Diesel jacket. Everyone around was staring at me. I put on my most nonchalant look while paddling furiously like a duck beneath my calm surface. When it began to rain, I couldn't get out to put up my manual car roof, which would hardly have helped anyway as it no longer attached to the windscreen, requiring me to hold it in place while I drove. So I simply slipped on the hood of my jacket, set my face like flint, and kept driving. No one would notice that the rain was pelting down as long as I didn't look like I noticed.

I was living my life hard, going at it like a bull gunning for red. As far as I was concerned, life had had a go at me and I wasn't going down without a fight. I kept my fists clenched, always ready to fight with life, with God, and with the growing ball of black gunk that threatened to upend my sanity. Self-control was all-important, and to hold off the rising pressure inside, I began to self-medicate with alcohol. I was a rebel with a cause, and I loved the adrenalin it gave me. I just didn't care, and no one could make me.

I never saw my mother now. I hardly spoke to her and had no desire to. Besides, although I wouldn't admit it, I was still afraid of her. So I never went back home to visit. How could I, when home represented all that I wanted to leave behind and forget, all the stuff I was determined to erase from my memory? I could never go back there. But the pain of my childhood kept bobbing its head above the deep waters I'd tried to drown it under. Whenever I washed myself in the shower, I felt like I was desperately trying to scrub off the humiliating memories of my childhood. So I drank myself into forgetfulness.

If my phone rang and I saw it was Mom, I got instant stomach cramps and nausea. Every word she spoke, every question she asked could be a fateful step on a landmine. And the anger and hurt, the shame, the total loss of control would flood through me when I thought about my conversations with her. As hard as I tried, I couldn't overcome the need and longing I still carried inside to be mothered. I ached for her approval. I wanted my mother to say sorry for all the things she'd done to me. I wanted her to say that I was enough just as I was. I wanted to hear her say, 'I love you.'

At times, when I felt strong enough, I tried to come up with ways of enticing my mother's acknowledgement and approval. I'd lavish her with gifts and money, or I'd go to excessive lengths to share my career, friendships and relationships with her. But it never resulted in the compassion I was hoping for. My mother couldn't be bribed into loving me. No amount of performance could garner any approval. Instead, the harder I tried, the more she withheld it from me, and the angrier I became.

My drinking got out of hand. My routine was to wake up, take a shower, put on my make-up and then medicate with copious amounts of red wine. The more I did this, the less I felt pleased or excited by anything I did. I was too anxious. A simple thing such as driving on the highway began to terrify me. My heart raced when my phone rang. I had become a fugitive, living like a hunted animal.

In 2001, a gossip article in the *City Press* newspaper published a fabricated story that I'd been rushed to hospital after passing out in my Beetle from a drug overdose. My mother called and I tried in vain to explain that it was all lies. To her it merely confirmed the beliefs she'd held about me all my life. Now that the whole world knew, she must have felt vindicated. It wasn't only my mother who didn't believe me. I was officially dubbed South Africa's baddest girl gone worse, and it seemed there was nothing I could do to clean up my reputation.

That night I lay awake in my apartment tormented by fear; afraid even to fall asleep. I knew at that moment that something was beginning to give. I felt the life slowly trickling out of me. I lay for hours on end, wracking my brain trying to figure out how they had ended up with a story like this. I tried to find traces of truth in the article that could perhaps have led to a trail of assumptions that culminated in this travesty. But there was none whatsoever. I felt like I had no lifeline.

At some point the words of Psalm 23 came into my head, and I crawled off my futon and went down on my knees. From the depths of my heart I cried out to God, who had always seemed so distant. I told him that if he cared at all, I needed him ASAP. Nothing particularly special happened, except that, for the first time in months, I fell sound asleep.

13

An Answered Prayer

THAT SAME WEEK I RECEIVED a call to say that the broadcaster would not be renewing the show's contract. I was shocked and demoralised. I had spent four years on *Technics Heart of the Beat*, and I couldn't believe it could end so abruptly. Deep inside, I'd outgrown it and I knew it was time for something else, but I hadn't yet come to terms with the idea.

A big chapter in my life was closing and I felt a deep sense of loss. I didn't feel ready to take the jump. I'd grown very close to the people I worked with, but not much was spoken about it among us; there was a shared understanding that the end of the road had come. It all ended very quietly and there was nobody to mourn with.

Panic set in. Where would my next job come from? I had

rent and bills to pay. I had finally got to that – I was now an adult with responsibilities.

I went to see my agent. Gaenor, after whom the agency was named, was a charismatic, fiercely opinionated lady who'd been a sought-after actress in her day. I loved her to bits, and she was good at what she did, though she did love to gossip with one artist about another. One of the bookers at her agency was Lisa Modisane, whom I'd gone to school with and had now grown fond of. I appreciated the encouragement and support she gave me. That day she told me about *Backstage*, a youth drama series that was shooting in Cape Town. They were on a highly publicised nationwide search for an actress to play the coveted role of Zandi, the new femme fatale; each day the top five auditions would be aired on national television so that the public could call in and vote for their favourite superbitch.

I was reluctant to enter such a public competition. I just wanted to get a job and move on; I wasn't up for the attention and hype, and this one was starting to look more like a beauty pageant than an audition. But Gaenor explained that it was the only way I could audition.

That night I prayed to God to rescue me. I prayed for a fresh start in life somewhere else, hopefully in another city where I could reinvent myself, away from the noise, media and public scrutiny.

After many auditions and much anticipation and anxiety, I was finally awarded the most sought-after role on South African television at the time, from among over thirty thousand entries.

During the auditioning period, I met Michael Strauss in Parkhurst one sunny afternoon, and he swept me off my already unstable feet. He was thirty-three, and ran a successful financial consultancy in Johannesburg.

Michael's love had a very calming effect on me; all he wanted to do was take care of me, and he'd say it often – no one had ever said such a thing to me before. He saw me as a fragile eagle with a broken wing, and made it his duty to nurse me back to health. In many ways, he did just that. This was one of the first times in my life I felt safe, loved and appreciated.

But when I arrived in Cape Town I was a wounded bird, barely surviving on a wing and a prayer. I was exhausted and scarcely alive. My bony frame was emaciated due to lack of appetite as a result of my reckless living. People thought I was confident, but I was acting, masking my shame. I was lonely, but I had my control to watch over it. I wouldn't dare expose the despair I'd come to know so well. Not ever. Yet it was impossible to keep up my guard all the time. Every now and then people would ask why I looked so tired and sad, and I'd quickly readjust my mask, for fear of being found out completely.

Backstage catapulted me to national fame. Everybody knew who Zandi was: she had become a formidable theatrical force in South Africa. Artistically, this was also the platform that birthed me as an actress. Here I faced the ultimate challenge of taking ownership and responsibility for the gift that had been thrust upon me at the bus stop that afternoon many years ago.

The *Backstage* crew welcomed me with mixed reactions. Some were excited and pleased to finally meet me, as most of them had grown up watching me on television. Others held their breath, expecting drama and intrigue, waiting to witness all the crazy stuff they'd heard about me. Most people there had preconceptions gathered from the media and the industry grapevine. I could tell that they thought I was a spoilt brat with an oversized ego and no respect for others. In their eyes I was the embodiment of a rebel and the ultimate prima donna.

This both amused and angered me. How had I reached this point? Who was this other Bonnie the world saw? It felt so far from the truth. But somehow I had grown accustomed to the labels and was subconsciously living up to their expectations of me. It was as if the media had successfully created a monster. And at times it was fun. I'd walk into a room and become aware that everyone was watching me, hawk-like, in anticipation of a drama. It was an invitation for me to act like the superbitch, and I was a willing pro. If it was a show they wanted, I'd give it to them in style.

But it was exhausting. In reality, all I wanted was to be treated like an ordinary person; to be loved unconditionally, to be given the benefit of the doubt. Except this isn't generally how the public engages with a famous personality. They don't try to look behind the persona that's been constructed in their individual and collective minds. Perhaps the real problem was that my mother had constructed her idea of me and had never tried to know me for who I was. The result was that I, myself, didn't recognise who I was beyond the roles that were thrust on me.

So there I was, feeling it again: that anxiety, that fear of falling; and a constant buzz as if adrenalin was being released intravenously in half-hourly spurts. I struggled to cope with anything unexpected, such as a last-minute arrangement or an extra guest rocking up without warning. I'd be completely thrown by the slightest deviation from a plan. If I was invited to a gathering by a friend, I wanted all the details of who would be present, so I had time to psyche myself up – what would be expected of Bonnie, how should I present her? And there were lots of events and gatherings. Later I would do a mental postmortem, scrutinising every conversation, every response I'd given, calculating people's opinions of me based on their facial expression: a smile, a frown, a silence, a glance when they thought I wasn't looking. I sifted through all of these as proof of whether I was liked or not – which was important to me, as long as the person didn't know.

Nevertheless, the serenity of Cape Town – as well as the fact that I was far from my mother – brought at least some relief. And the ravenous Johannesburg tabloids were far away, as most weren't in circulation in the Mother City.

Among the cast of *Backstage*, I quickly became friends with a very special young lady, Marubini Mogale, who played the role of Irene. She was gentle and generous, and we connected from the first moment we spoke to each other. Most people in the cast wondered how an angel like her could stomach a wild child like me. Unexpectedly, my friendship with Marubini did a lot towards healing me. Her willingness to continue our friendship, no matter what people said about me, made me want to try again and give life a bit more enthusiasm. Just by accepting me as a friend, she made me feel that maybe, just maybe, the labels my mother and the media had stuck on me were untrue. She reminded me of an innocence I'd misplaced, and gave me hope that I could recover it again. We shared endless daydreaming sessions about Hollywood and the Oscars we'd win, and in her presence I lost my jadedness and remembered how it felt to be a child in a playground. Our friendship helped me dare to believe that I, too, was deserving of loyalty, love and unconditional acceptance. She was fair, honest and never afraid to disagree with me. She always gave people the benefit of the doubt, and saw the world through eyes of faith.

Vusi's mother, Shado, was living in Cape Town, and two

months after my arrival there, I gave her a call to say hello. I had remained in touch with her, as she still had a special place in my heart. She was very interested to hear how I was doing. She missed me, she said, and invited me to come and live with her.

'Come home,' she said simply, and her words touched me. I was intending to move out of the expensive Sea Point flat I had taken temporarily while I got settled, and I was grateful to find a familiar face and space in Cape Town. Perhaps subconsciously I even hoped it could help rekindle my romance with Vusi, since I wasn't completely over him. So I moved in with Shado and Vusi's younger sister, Owami.

It was indeed like being home, and it kept me out of trouble. I could look forward to a home-cooked meal every night. Owami and I had always got on well, and our relationship thrived. Shado was a great friend and mother figure to me, and we loved each other's company. Her house was a vibrant hub of music, culture and famous people.

While I was staying there, Miriam Makeba came to stay so she could spend a few peaceful days away with her grandson. She was a fine cook, and I loved to be in the presence of these two great ladies as they shared remarkable and hilarious tales of their travels and the famous people who were part of their lives. They inspired me with their knowledge of the world and all things cultured and artistic, as well as their interesting attire and jewellery from places I'd never even heard of. I wanted to be like them.

As I was the youngster in the house, Mama Miriam sometimes sent me on errands for her, and I was honoured. One day as I set out to drop off an outfit for her at the hotel where she'd be performing that evening, she asked me for my phone number so she could call me later. I confessed shyly that I'd recently lost my phone.

'What?' she said. 'What's a beautiful young girl like you doing without a cellphone; how do you expect your suitors to contact you?' As I giggled, she took a wad of cash from her purse and told me to go and get myself a phone. I was certainly living an interesting life.

Every now and then the landline would ring, and I'd answer, only for my heart to leap at the sound of Vusi's voice. We'd chat briefly and then I'd pass the phone to his mom. After a few months, the familiar heartbreak began to settle over me as it sank in that there was no hope of recovering our lost love. Being in such close proximity to everything that represented Vusi wasn't wise, I realised, and I couldn't keep loving him this way; it was unhealthy.

One morning as I sat sipping coffee on the balcony as I waited for my lift to work, watching the sun creep over the waterfront like a lover, I was startled by the flapping of wings. I turned to see a panicked sparrow fluttering around the lounge, trying to find a way out through the glass doors. I watched for a bit, not sure how to help, then gently opened the glass doors wider. As it suddenly found its escape and flew out, I realised what it was I needed to do.

It broke my heart to say goodbye to this beautiful place and these special people with whom I felt so at home, but for my own wellbeing, I knew I had to go. Shado was compassionate and I knew she understood, but I felt too awkward to explain all the crazy emotions that were overwhelming me, so I poured my heart out in a letter and moved out while she was at work. Marubini helped me pack and put me up for about a week while I looked for a new spot.

I found a flat in Orange Street in Gardens. Finally I had my heart back, and all that was left to do was nurse it back to health. Shado and I later had a peaceful conversation, which smoothed things over.

Compared to Johannesburg, Cape Town was old-money country, and South Africa's bastion of white supremacy. You hardly saw a black person in the city; they seemed to be a forgotten people, all tucked away in decaying settlements far away from the centre, the beachfronts or the winding Garden Route. As a game, I'd count the number of black faces I'd seen during the past day, and I never got higher than five. Walking into a restaurant was met by what-are-you-doing-here stares, as if questioning my very existence. But I refused to be rattled by it, and enjoyed flaunting my black skin wherever I went, proud to be black among a sea of disapproving white faces. After all, that's what I did, I stood out. And besides, I was dating a white guy.

Michael would fly down to Cape Town to see me from time to time. It was always a treat when he came; we'd have fun sightseeing and doing all the touristy things. His parents, who also lived in Cape Town, weren't at all pleased that he was dating a black girl; in fact, they were horrified. His father refused to meet me, but his mother, out of politeness and love for her son, agreed to meet me in the Gardens Centre, a quaint little shopping mall on Orange Street within walking distance of my flat. She and I were both wracked with nerves as we sat there sipping coffee. Some of her gym buddies happened by and stopped to say hello, throwing questioning glances in my direction, awaiting an explanation for my presence. 'This is Michael's, ah, *friend*,' she stuttered more than once. I smiled sweetly and waved, amused at the irony that on that day, more gym buddies than she could have expected happened to pass our table. But silently I commended her. She was doing what a loving mother did – biting the bullet and showing some support.

I never did meet Michael's father, except by a mischievous act of nature. One morning, in the Virgin Active gym in Green Point, as I stood fixing the bike settings before a vigorous spinning session, none other than Michael's father walked up to take the bike beside mine. I recognised him from the photos in Michael's album, and we spun side by side for the next hour, I with the smuggest smile while I panted for breath. I didn't say anything to him, but I shared the story with Michael, who found it most amusing.

Cape Town for me was a much-needed time away from the spotlight and media scrutiny. It gave me a chance to discover parts of me I didn't know and rediscover those that I'd lost in the whirlwind that had become my life. Socially, Cape Town welcomed individuality; the youth were very experimental and pushed the boundaries of artistic expression at work and in fashion. It was a place where strange fruit could thrive, and I did. Where Johannesburg was a drive-thru McDonald's McMuffin meal on your way to work through profanity-inducing traffic, Cape Town was a hearty breakfast with good coffee while staring dreamily at the mountain.

In this blissful atmosphere came a painful realisation: I'd become estranged from my brother and sister through my attempt to flee as far as possible from the responsibilities I'd carried at home for what felt like my whole existence. I missed them and wondered about them now that they were out of reach. How were they faring? I'd seen them both from time to time, but had missed a big chunk of their formative years. I felt guilty for not having been there to protect and help them through some of the fiercest years of my mother's melancholy. I'd left them to fight the same wars that had scarred me, which I'd miraculously survived. Now that I was in Cape Town, I wanted to connect with them and make amends for what I could neither explain nor fix. I wanted to instil in them a hope for the future, a sense that one day the pain would be over and they too would be free. I also wanted them to know that I'd tried really hard to rescue them, but that it had all become just too much for me.

So I organised with my mother for them to take a bus to Cape Town and spend the school holidays with me. I lavished them with gifts and packed our time together with many fun-filled activities. We went to movies, played games and took long walks in the park. My brother had developed a colourful sense of humour, and we enjoyed laughing at his jokes. My sister was very willing and always trying to help with the chores in the flat.

Yet we couldn't fill the loneliness that hung between us; we'd been apart for so long it felt like we had oceans to swim to reach each other. Maybe I felt it more than they did. I felt a pressing need to explain why our childhood had played out the way it did, and that it wasn't that they were bad or unlovable children. But words failed me. There were many strained silences between us, many unspoken things. I was still very angry at my mother at that time, and had to fight hard to not let my anger spew out whenever her name came up.

It was sweet to see my brother's protectiveness towards my sister, and how my sister looked up to me as her heroine. But a part of me wanted to tell her not to emulate me. I was so broken and she still so pure and innocent; I wanted her to find her own way, not turn out like me. By the time my brother and sister left for Jo'burg, we had gained some ground between us, and we all looked forward to more time together in future.

One Sunday morning, Marubini and I, both hungry for a spiritual anchor, took up an invitation from Maria, our make-up artist, to visit His People Church in Rondebosch. That day, both our lives changed. My dam wall broke in the midst of hundreds of Jesus-crazy students during worship. Not even my awkwardness could stop me. All the tears I'd never shed were now pouring down my cheeks, and there was nothing I could do to resist them or preserve my dignity. I had no control.

I encountered God that morning in a way that opened my heart to a whole new world, a deep knowing that he really cared and wanted to be a part of my life. From that day on, I became a regular at the church. I joined their Bible School and got to know Jesus as a friend, an ever-present brother. My healing had begun.

Since then I've always associated the Mother City with hope, restoration and rest. It's a place I call home; it speaks my heart, and I continue to long for Cape Town's nurturing arms. There, in its tranquillity, at a distance from the chaos of my childhood, I tried to understand why my mother had hurt me so badly, why she couldn't love me. I tried in my limited way to piece together the threads of her life and account for the pain and the rage that she had offloaded onto me.

One morning I was given a lift to church by one of the congregation, Liezl Ackerman. We started chatting in her car, and instantly connected. Soon we were inseparable. Liezl was a preschool teacher who spoke of the children she taught as though they were her own. As I came to know the events that had shaped Liezl's life, I learnt a lot about forgiveness. Her mother had been among those gunned down during the infamous St James church massacre in 1993. Had she not spent the previous night at a friend's house, she too would have been in the church when the attack happened. During her struggle to come to terms with the anguish, Liezl had finally mustered the guts to confront her mother's murderers in prison. She had looked them in the eye, described to them what it had done to her family, and then told them that she forgave them. She spoke of those boys with a compassion that made me marvel; it was the greatest story of forgiveness I'd ever heard. In my own battle to forgive, Liezl's story provided inspiration I badly needed.

At the end of that year, Marubini was killed in a car accident. The devastating news rocked everyone at *Backstage*. Her loss echoed deeply inside me, bringing with it the cold breeze of abandonment. Once again, I was lost, left behind.

My friendships with fellow cast members Grace Mahlaba and Sibusiso Hadebe, who played the mother and the nephew, now became my source of strength at work. Together we found comfort in each other's memories of Marubini, a beautiful soul whose love we were all grateful to have known. I will always miss Marubini.

14

Facing the Music

Soon after the loss of Marubini, the management of *Backstage* changed hands, and our shooting location was moved to Johannesburg.

The history I'd left behind in Jozi came rushing back to meet me like a welcoming committee, and the old Bonnie resurfaced on the faces of my friends. I tried to explain how I'd changed, that I'd found God and become a born-again Christian, but no one was having it. Some thought it was hogwash, and others were amused at the absurdity of me keeping it up. They clung to the Bonnie they supposedly knew, and I couldn't convince them otherwise. So once more I began acting the old Bonnie, although I continued to go to church every Sunday. But I found it increasingly difficult to live out my spiritual convictions and subsequent lifestyle choices within the circles I'd enjoyed before moving to Cape Town.

After a couple of months of a double life, I knew something had to give. I was left with two options: convert all my friends to my new way of life, or change my friendship circle completely. It wasn't that I disliked my friends, or that we no longer had anything in common. But I saw the world with new eyes now, and I was desperate to find answers and seek the truth. My urgency was driving me down a different path, which I was happy to take.

My first priority on moving back to Johannesburg was to plant myself in a church, so I looked up His People Church in Johannesburg and made a point of settling in. I always felt safest in the back row. There I felt invisible, witnessing all that went on at the front without feeling the pressure to do as the Romans do. Besides, I disliked being stared at, and at my particular church people did more staring than churching. They must have wondered what I was doing there in the first place, and thought that staring would help them figure it out. My face gave nothing away, but I found it rather uncomfortable to stare back. The braver ones would sometimes come over and express gratitude to God for saving me, urging me to bring 'all the other TV people' to church, because they seemed in great need of salvation. They probably had a point, but I didn't like the implication that artists were somehow greater sinners just because they were artists.

I didn't get close to anyone, and held the entire congregation at arm's length. I was trying to find something, knocking and seeking. I was looking for peace of mind, I suppose. I wanted to accept myself for who I really was, but I thought then that I needed to change first before God could accept me. By going to church, I was committing to work hard at changing to become a good, un-awkward, happy Christian.

But I didn't trust these church people. I was suspicious of their friendliness, and found them nosy and overbearing. They smiled too much and asked personal questions, and I immediately questioned their motives. But I stuck around. Somehow, every Sunday I experienced a certain peace, an okayness with myself and the world. I hoped that in this way I could live a reasonably normal life and become reasonably happy with myself.

To avoid the questions and those overzealous smiles, my trick was to arrive just after the service had begun, and leave as soon as the pastor began to dismiss the congregation. That way I could keep my peace, and avoid becoming annoyed and losing it. I'd scurry off to my car, avoiding eye contact all the way. Sometimes, of course, I'd be ambushed by a brave person with a huge smile and an eager hug. To escape, I'd lie about some important thing I had to rush off and do.

Running off from church required a lot of concentration and planning. I'd carefully watch and wait for just the right moment. Sometimes I'd misjudge and leave it a little too late, by which time it would be too awkward. So I'd sit there, trapped, my throat bloated with a fear of condemnation that I couldn't seem to swallow and move beyond. The congregation would be looking at me, reading my evil thoughts. I wanted to hide.

I just couldn't believe all that stuff they said with their full-toothed smiles. The goodness of the church was too much for me. I was more of a sinner than the rest of them put together. I was dripping in shame, convinced that the others were just born squeaky clean and holy. But I had to clutch onto this fragile peace I'd found, and if it meant pretending to be a cookie-cutter version of everybody there, then that's what I would do. Once again, I was living a double life. And I couldn't bear it.

Sitting in the back row one Sunday morning, I prayed to God to help me get the whole church thing. Nothing happened. Perhaps I wasn't asking the right question, wasn't ready to be honest about what was really going on. I wanted the peace, but I didn't want to let go of the things that were holding me back, because I'd found my identity and security in them. I shuddered at the thought of opening up to strangers about things not even my mother knew – revealing my fears, insecurities, skeletons and shady past to strangers.

But if this was really what it would take to embrace the truth, I was game to give it a try. It didn't happen overnight, but very, very gradually I began to open my heart, accept invitations to lunches and open up about my life to a few people. It seemed impossible to get to know God without experiencing the people he'd placed around me. And I began to receive the love, the hugs and the prayers.

Slowly but surely I began to feel at home, like I belonged. The church became my community, the hospital I sought. There I found the fathers and sisters I had longed for, a place where I could just be. Here I learnt that if I let go, I had nothing to hide or be ashamed of. This was not a place where perfect people gathered; it was a place where the broken gathered to hold each other up, give encouragement, and help lift each other's heads up towards a God who loves. I continued to arrive afraid, presenting myself before my father along with his many other children.

I gradually began to understand how church fitted into my relationship with God. Was it necessary? Yes. Was it perfect? No. It finally dawned on me that church was more about getting together with like-minded people and celebrating the perfection of the one we'd chosen to lavish our affection on. It wasn't about our own perfection – we had none to speak of. We were like-minded in that we'd all fallen in love with Jesus Christ, and needed each other for support, encouragement and companionship along our path to knowing God better and loving him more. For too long I had judged church and Christians according to how well they behaved, when it was never about them in the first place. It was about God, his love and his goodness, and the amazing, mindboggling truth that he has room in his heart for all of us, whatever our shape, size or colour; that he is totally accepting of all our diversity.

This realisation made it easier for me to open up to the people around me. I knew some of them would fail me or disappoint me, or behave in ways that were contrary to our understanding of Jesus, but I knew I would too, and I found solace in the fact that my faith was in an unchanging God. There will always be annoying people at church, but the reality is that I, too, have annoying tendencies of my own that I expect others to put up with.

15

Dipping and Soaring

THE MOVE BACK TO JOHANNESBURG had been abrupt. Fast-and-furious Jozi was a rude awakening from my Cape Town slumber, where life had moved at a slower pace and there'd been time to stop and ponder the beauty of a flower or a rock. It was as if in Cape Town more space existed between the seconds and minutes, unlike in the concrete jungle of Jo'burg.

The weight of the role of Zandi had grown heavier and more difficult. Zandi's constant manipulation, lying and plotting against everyone started to influence my behaviour offset. The boundary between my personality and Zandi's was steadily eroding, and inhabiting her unstable ways while trying to keep a lid on my own unresolved anger, anxiety and resentment became a recipe for disaster. Meditating on Zandi's destructive thoughts and words in order to deliver a convincing performance was shaking my own demons loose.

After one of many arguments with an intoxicated crew member on set, I was called into the producer's office and reprimanded. The producer refused to hear my side of the story and sided with the drunken crew member. As I voiced my unhappiness in the meeting, she said, 'If you don't like it, leave.'

'Oh? Then I quit,' I retorted. I submitted my resignation the following morning.

I found myself caught up in a maelstrom of frustration and confusion. The combined effects of the death of Marubini, the sudden move to Johannesburg with its proximity to my mother, and my constant portrayal of Zandi's psychotic character were propelling me rapidly towards a meltdown. So many emotions and memories had surfaced that I began to doubt the benefit of staying in Jo'burg.

My emotional recovery became a priority, and so I asked my mother for a meeting. I knew she would struggle to hear what I had to say, but I felt I had to tell her how the events of my childhood had affected me. No matter how much I talked it over with close friends and church counsellors, sharing it with her seemed even more important for my healing. I knew she couldn't change what had happened, but trying to protect her from the responsibility of owning it was hurting me too much.

It was one of the most difficult conversations I've ever had. It ended up taking place in a car in the parking lot of Southgate Mall, and perhaps it was the best place. Here we were in close proximity, but she couldn't shut any doors, walk out, or claim later that she hadn't heard.

Convulsing with tears, I described event after event in

detail, the things that were said, the insults that affected my identity, and how each had made me feel and were still affecting my view of the world and myself. I explained that I needed to return to their source in order to heal, that I'd forgiven her, and that I loved her very much. I just needed her to own these things and acknowledge the devastation they'd left behind.

My mother denied everything. She accused me of dreaming up ways to discredit her and make her look like a monster. I was ungrateful. She had raised me all by herself, fed me, given me an education and done everything for me. Was this now what she could expect in return? God would rescue her from this web of lies I had spun about her, she cried.

I walked away with the sinking realisation that neither my mother nor anyone else was ever going to account for what had happened during my childhood. I had to simply forgive her for all she'd done, and for what she was still doing and would continue to do. I had to find my own closure.

I could either be a victim of my past or a victor in my unfolding future. I decided I had to find my own way to win, to live and to leave it all behind, so that I could keep exploring the great opportunities that life was presenting to me.

16

Cleaning Up

WITH SO MUCH UPHEAVAL OVER the previous few months, it was time to brave whatever lay before me. I moved in with Michael and bought myself an Opel Corsa with a lump-sum payout from an old MTN commercial. I felt like I was starting over again.

My departure from *Backstage* had created a lot of media buzz. Unfortunately, some individuals from its production company, the Moja Movie Factory, fed the media with vitriolic accusations and exaggerated accounts of my prima donna ways – I was a lunatic, and they were the victims of my disruptive ways.

Michael was very supportive during this time, and kept reminding me of how unhappy I'd been while on *Backstage*.

Only good could come out of this, he told me. I was home all day with little to do, so I spent my time regrouping and getting my ducks in a row. I left Gaenor and scouted for an agent better equipped to handle the direction I wanted to take, which was strictly acting. I was no longer afraid of calling myself an actress, and owning that title without cringing or doubting whether I had the goods.

I got signed with a new agent, Penny Charteris, a very proper Englishwoman who'd been a sought-after actress in her prime, and was fond of her gin and tonics, her dogs and her actors. She related to the actors she represented like her own brood of children, and she nurtured and scolded whenever she needed to. Penny sat me down and set me straight, saying that she believed I was beautiful and talented, but to get serious I needed to tone down my fiery personality.

I continued going to church and getting used to this new church family. Although it was part of the same body of churches, it had a different personality. I was also still weaning myself off my old Jozi crowd.

Michael had a vague notion of God, but wasn't a fan of church. I couldn't hold that against him, but I was coming to realise that it would be difficult to fully immerse myself in the waters of my faith while holding his hand. Our relationship was going reasonably well, but we didn't share the same values. I'd wake up to go to church on Sunday, and he'd either drop me off or stay behind. But I wanted to pursue God and see him in all his glory, because if he'd created me for a purpose, he alone knew how I was designed to work and thrive.

I also no longer wanted to have sex with someone who wasn't my husband. It felt like I was giving too much away, because as I got to understand God's original design for the family, I saw how I was using sex as a comfort, meeting a demand from my hormones. I'd never given it much thought, just done what I saw done. But now I couldn't ignore the emptiness I felt afterwards. I wanted the person I was sharing my body with to honour it as the special gift it was, not just dismiss it as another woman they'd had. I also began to wonder how many people I'd have to sleep with before I met the one I was going to be with forever. The idea of just clocking up my sex logbook disgusted me. It seemed so futile and aimless, as well as costly, because it was eroding something inside me.

When I'd first read in the Bible of God's disapproval of sex outside marriage, I thought it was a lot for God to ask, and that the world had changed too much since he'd put that expectation out there. But here I was now, feeling this erosion, longing to have this part of me cherished in a forever agreement. I'd heard many girls my age speak of the same thing, both Christians and non-Christians; it seemed to be the deep cry of every woman's heart. My journey with God was causing me to reconsider my world views. Much of what I had come to accept I had assimilated without prior consent from myself. Now I was going back to the drawing board and tracing my way back through the experiences and ideas that had framed and fashioned my thinking. I had conversations with Michael about how I was feeling, but he vehemently disagreed with me, claiming that church had brainwashed me.

Eight months went by before I worked again. I was cast in the second season of *Gaz'lam* directed by Alex Yazbek, where I played an HIV-positive young woman. *Gaz'lam* was part of a new wave of television series sweeping the industry, of real stories shot in a raw and gritty style, void of the usual unrelenting fluffiness. Although I felt rusty after not having worked for so long, it was a pleasant experience that I thoroughly enjoyed. My relationship with Michael was on its last legs, and it was clear that we didn't have a future together. I'd taken a turn in the path, and our views were now fundamentally different on most things. So as soon as shooting was wrapped on *Gaz'lam*, I moved out.

After staying temporarily with a friend, I decided I no longer wanted to live on my own. I'd lived alone since I was eighteen, and now, at twenty-five, I moved in with an Afrikaans-speaking graphic designer called Eben. He was an excellent cook, had great taste in music and quirky tastes in most other things. We got on famously.

In the second half of that year I was cast in a film called *Drum*. The story focused on the life and times of Sophiatown and the legacy of *Drum* magazine, culminating in the forced removals of Sophiatown's inhabitants. My role was a character based on the musical icon Dolly Rathebe, and I played alongside Taye Diggs, Tumisho Masha, Fezile Mpela, Zola 7, Keke Semoko and other great South African performers. It was to be my first cinematic role.

Being on set was nerve-wracking. I was working among highly respected artists, and playing a real person added pressure; I really wanted to do her justice and portray her in the best possible way. As she was a singer, I had to mime her performances, typically in a shebeen or at events where all the other characters would be watching. All eyes would be on me, and I was required to dance and beguile them with my presence. The challenge was also greater because she wasn't just a conventional character – her personality was in some ways quite over the top. I often wished for the earth to open up and swallow me, it was so tough. But the challenge was good for me. The main shooting was wrapped after two months, followed by a couple of months of post-production.

The following year, we got word that *Drum* was being well received worldwide, and the producers had decided we should tour the film festivals. So in 2003 I set out on my first-ever trip outside of the country. Our first stop was Toronto, followed by London and Cannes, and the following year we did the Munich film festival. Attending these events was a dream come true, and a truly mind-blowing experience for me. The premiere of *Drum* took place in Toronto, and the excitement among the cast, director and producers was tremendous. I appeared on the red carpet in a gorgeous black-and-yellow ensemble from Stoned Cherrie, with my head clean shaven. This caused some shock, and Taye Diggs leaned over to ask if I was sick. Annoyed, I gave him a sharp answer about him being such a typical American. I felt a bit like a deer caught in the headlights, but worked hard to look like I was having the time of my life.

The best was when the lights went out. Getting to watch myself on the big screen for the first time was a powerful experience. It was also exhilarating being introduced to thousands of applauding film enthusiasts from all over the world. There were also plenty of interviews with TV, radio and print media, and no shortage of events and dinners to attend. I loved dressing up in my Stoned Cherrie outfits and being the exotic, bald-headed African girl in the room. Everyone wondered where in the world I was from, and I even overheard a comment from Kevin Spacey saying that he found me beautiful.

On my return, my agent got me an audition for the Danish film, *Blinded Angels*, playing a domestic worker whose blind employer falls madly in love with her. It was a beautiful art piece with slow-moving shots and a poetic script, which we shot in Hout Bay. While we were shooting, my agent called to say that the well-known Australian director, Phillip Noyce, wanted me to read the script for a film called *Catch a Fire*. The script was delivered to me on set, and I fell instantly in love with it.

Nervously, I went to meet Phillip Noyce at the Mount Nelson Hotel – his achievements by then included *Clear and Present Danger, The Saint, Sliver* and *Rabbit-Proof Fence*.

He met me in the lobby and escorted me to the meeting room, where Robyn Slovo, daughter of Joe Slovo, was one of the producers. They asked what I thought of the film and discussed their expectations of the role, then asked me to read a scene from the script that I'd prepared.

When I was done, Phillip Noyce had a satisfied smile, like he'd found the right match. They said they'd be back the following year to finalise the castings. I left the Mount Nelson with a big smile, surprised at the way God had orchestrated my leap into film acting.

I wrapped the shooting of *Blinded Angels* and spent the Christmas holidays in Cape Town with my friend Liezl Ackerman. Christmas lunch with her family was a treat. Her father was a charismatic actor and businessman, and entertained us with funny stories. I loved the sweet potatoes, which were made the good, old-fashioned Afrikaner way and drenched in a sweet sauce by his new wife, Anne. After lunch, we opened presents over coffee and wine, and later, when we started to feel peckish, Mr Ackerman made delicious cheese melts with lots of butter, sliced tomatoes, and tomato sauce underneath the melting cheese.

Soon afterwards I received a call from Phillip Noyce, reassuring me that he'd loved my audition. This encouraged me, because I couldn't get it out of my mind. Early the following year, in 2005, Penny called to tell me to get my passport ready. I was to fly to London for a callback audition for the role of Precious in *Catch a Fire*. Just days later, Terry

Pheto and I found ourselves on a plane to London, where we would both audition for the same role.

London was cold and drizzly, and we spent the day in our respective hotel rooms preparing for our auditions the following day. That evening we had dinner with Phillip, Robyn and Suzy Figgus at the Ivy Restaurant near Covent Garden, a restaurant popular with celebrities and theatregoers. The dinner was relaxed and fun, although I was conscious that this was also part of the audition. Phillip dared us to try a dish we'd never had before, so I ordered lobster.

The next morning my nerves were a tangle of spaghetti. I was called in first. I'd hoped it would be just me and a camera, but in the room were Robyn, Suzy and Phillip. As always, I gave it everything I had. As I turned to leave, Phillip reached for a copy of his autobiography, *Backroads to Hollywood*, penned a message on the inside cover and handed it to me.

Walking back to the taxi, tears welled up in my eyes as I read his words. 'To Bonnie, who will soar higher than all of us. Phillip Noyce.'

17

A Lesson in Love

EARLY ONE MORNING AFTER RETURNING from London, I received a call from Sisanda Henna, an acquaintance who'd been calling sporadically over the past two years, either to congratulate me on recent work or just to chat.

At first I was a bit baffled by these innocent chats in which he never flirted or suggested a date – it seemed that he just wanted a phone buddy. But on this particular morning, he asked me out for dinner.

'When?' I asked.

'Tonight.'

I agreed, and went back to sleep.

Sisanda was a very attractive Xhosa actor whose work I admired, so when I had bumped into him at a shop in Melville two years earlier, we'd greeted politely and flirted a little as I complimented him on his recent lead role in the TV drama series *Tsha Tsha*. Seeing him in the flesh had confirmed that everything about him was lead material; he was tall and well built with a boyish charm, an unquenchable enthusiasm and a smile that set his eyes twinkling. Two months later I encountered him at the Selimathunzi Duku Duku awards ceremony, where he received an award and gave a brief acceptance speech. He looked dashing, to say the least. After the ceremony I strolled over to where he stood, among a throng of mainly female admirers, and congratulated him, adding that I thought it was well deserved. A month or so later I accompanied a girlfriend to the Style Awards evening as she'd been nominated for an award. Sisanda was also a nominee – for Most Stylish Man in a TV Series. He didn't win that night, but he did score my phone number after chatting up a storm all evening, and again at breakfast the next morning. Not that we spent the night together; all guests and their partners had received a complimentary night at the hotel, so my friend and I had joined his group at breakfast the following morning.

Sisanda began calling me occasionally after that, but never once alluded to any desire to see or pursue me. Not until now. As we sat at the pizzeria on Oxford Road opposite my apartment block, we chatted and laughed with ease, as always. When I asked why he'd taken so long to ask me out, he explained that he'd been in a relationship and madly in love, and had no intention of cheating on her. But now they'd broken up. His gentleman score shot into double digits that very moment, though of course I didn't tell him this. He was polite, unconventional and charming, and I liked him a lot.

After dinner we took a walk around the block. Then, since my place was right across the street, I invited him in for coffee.

We sat on the balcony chatting, but when he leaned towards me for a kiss, I backed away in shock. He was equally shocked by my reaction. He didn't know that after I'd broken up with Michael I'd decided to remain celibate until my husband showed. Since then I'd fallen off the wagon occasionally, but each time I dusted myself off and kept going, and it became easier. I was no longer willing to have sex with anyone until we'd walked down the aisle. I'd grown tired of the relationship merry-go-round and was ready for commitment. But I didn't tell him all this. All I said was that I was uncomfortable about him trying to kiss me on the first date.

Insulted, he declared that our evening was over. Awkwardly, I still had to drive him home, since a driver had brought him to work and later dropped him at my place for our date. During the drive we barely spoke, and I could feel his ego spitting fire. But the trip was mercifully short.

I thought I'd seen the last of him that night. To my surprise, he called the next day, asking me along to watch Freshlyground perform at the newly refurbished Constitution Hill. We had fun and I went home convinced I'd fallen for this guy. Thandiswa had to stop me going on and on about him; I started driving all my friends crazy.

After our third date, things were heating up and we ended up kissing. A few moments into the kiss I stopped him, knowing that if I didn't, I'd find myself naked in his bed. I'd let it go too far; my own heart had betrayed me.

'What's wrong?' he asked.

I apologised for leading him on, and explained my convictions about intimacy, marriage, relationships and God. He was not only shocked but annoyed with me, and became very dismissive. Actually, it was fine with him, he said, because he was still in love with his ex and he still wanted it to work out with her.

119

I walked to my car with a mixture of anger and relief. Anger because I would have been just another conquest to help him lick the wounds of his past relationship, and relief because I'd finally had a revelation of God's protective nature. Avoiding sex before marriage was not just an outdated religious law but had proven its value. It had protected me from things that weren't obvious to me at first. I was grateful for the whole experience, and wouldn't have changed anything about it.

But when I got to my car I said a quick prayer. 'God, please can you fix this? Can you put us on the same page and make this work? Please can you make this guy my husband, because he's a lovely guy and I really like him.'

I didn't think too much about the incident again. Nearly four months later, Sisanda called to ask me to the theatre. I told him I didn't think it was a good idea, in light of how things had ended the last time. But he interrupted me. It was really important that we meet, he said. As he drove us to the theatre that night, something was different about him. He was very calm, not putting on the cool act most guys do on a date. He wasn't even doing the gangster lean; he had his seat in a comfortable position and seemed to really be listening to me.

We saw *Tshepang*, a heartwrenching story about the rape of a baby, starring one of my favourite actors, Mncedisi Shabangu. As we sat sipping coffee afterwards, I noticed more changes in Sisanda. Something drastic and significant had taken place here. But I didn't want to fall for this guy all over again, so I did my best to keep up my guard.

On the drive home, he explained that since we'd last seen each other, he'd got back together with his girlfriend, but when things didn't work out again, he'd fallen into a deep depression as issues from his past began to resurface. A friend of his – Cumani Booi, who played professional rugby for the Lions – persuaded him to come to church. After standing Cumani up a few times, the day he finally went changed his life. He had an encounter with God similar to the one I'd had in Cape Town years ago.

I couldn't believe what I was hearing. My thoughts rushed back to my prayer that night in the car. Could this really be happening? But he was still speaking, and I needed to pay attention. Since his encounter with God, he'd remembered the genuineness of my faith and its impact on him. He wanted to spend more time with me, as he had many questions to ask and wanted to grow in his own faith. But this time, he added, he was only interested in friendship, and he apologised for trying to get into my pants last time. I had to pinch myself, it felt so surreal.

We began to spend a lot of time together. We would share deep things, and at times even go to church together. He definitely behaved like someone who was truly interested in friendship. His eyes didn't rove up and down my body as we spoke any more; instead he looked me squarely in the eye. Our friendship progressed calmly, and our feelings resurfaced as the time we spent together grew.

Sisanda was planning a move to the United States. He'd been offered a partial scholarship to study film-making at the University of Southern California, and he planned to first work for three months in New Jersey as a facilitator at a summer camp for troubled inner-city kids. He spent much of his time applying for scholarships, and I offered any help I could. Once again I was drawn to him but, with the knowledge that he'd soon be leaving, I was trying hard to keep up my guard.

Three weeks before his departure, he took a trip to the Eastern Cape to drop off a few items for storage at his parents' home. As soon as he reached their home, he called me in excitement.

'You won't believe this,' he said. 'It's the weirdest thing!'

'What?' I asked impatiently.

'I just walked into my father's bedroom, and there's a framed picture of the two of us on his dresser!'

This was indeed crazy. His father didn't know me from a bar of soap, and Sisanda had never mentioned me in any of their conversations. The picture had been taken a couple of weeks earlier at the premiere of the movie *U-Carmen eKhayelitsha*. What made it even stranger, he explained, was that whenever his father came across a photo of Sisanda with others, he always cut them out of the picture to leave only his son, especially if they were girls he didn't know. So Sisanda was truly astounded, and took it very seriously. He felt it was some sort of prophetic message.

When Sisanda returned to Johannesburg, we went to see his pastor to help us figure out what it was we needed to do, especially in light of his pending travels. His pastor was very frank with us. She explained that we needed to pray and ask God if we were each other's life partners before deciding to act on our feelings, so as not to waste each other's time dating and stringing each other along.

'Ask God if you're meant to marry each other. I doubt he'll be trying to keep it from you. So just ask.'

We left feeling overwhelmed. We'd gone there to ask advice about our developing relationship, and left with the task of asking God if we were each other's spouses. Needless to say, the atmosphere on the drive home was uncomfortable, although, in some ways, things were simpler now.

The remaining two weeks of Sisanda's stay in Johannesburg were quite emotional. We tried to squeeze in as much time together as possible, as we dreaded parting.

But each time we looked at each other, we wondered if the other had received an answer yet. Sisanda hadn't secured funds for the remainder of the costs that the scholarship didn't cover, and all doors seemed to be shut, so he wasn't going to be able to do the course. But he'd decided to do the summer camp anyway. Sisanda loved kids and had the biggest, kindest heart – qualities that really drew me to him.

'Oh, can't God just write it in the clouds?' he said in frustration one day. 'I've asked him but I still haven't heard a thing.'

'He could, I guess. He's God after all,' I mumbled. I had asked a pastor and a couple of other people at church how I could tell if God's answer was a yes or a no. They all told me the same thing. You'll sense overwhelming peace whenever it's a yes, they said, and an unsettling doubt if it's a no. The trick was to be still enough to listen and hear, by spending time praying and talking to him about it, to avoid the trap of doing whatever my head told me.

So I already knew Sisanda was the man I wanted to marry. I had a deep knowing in my soul that settled like a pendulum swinging in perfect balance, comfortable and at ease. But I wasn't going to tell him. It would be too humiliating if he didn't have the same conviction, so I kept it to myself.

The two weeks flew by, and we said nothing more about it to each other. The day of his departure arrived, and I drove him to the airport. When we arrived there, I waited for him to finish checking in, then walked him to the boarding gate. The time had come to say goodbye. He hugged me, gave me a light peck on the lips, and finally looked me in the eye.

'I know you're my wife,' he said. 'When I come back, I'm gonna marry you.' He gave me one long, final hug, turned around and strode off into the distance.

I stood there for a good five minutes, unable to wipe the smile off my face.

We spent the next three months emailing, Skyping and instant messaging. The longing caused by the distance and absence bound us together and, ironically, brought us closer, and our emails were filled with love and sweet, tender words.

While he was away, my time was filled with preparations for my role in *Catch a Fire*. This would be my biggest film role so far, and I was working with very talented people. My character, Precious, was very intense, complex and damaged in many ways. She was silent in most of her scenes, which was challenging; with so little dialogue, I had to get more creative in my nonverbal interpretation and capitalise more on body language. I read through the script over and over again, familiarising myself with my character's world, listening to the music of the period, interviewing women who'd been through similar experiences during the struggle and reading all I could lay my hands on about that period. Preparation for a role was always nerve-wracking, because each time there came a point where I wasn't sure I'd be able to pull it off. Well before filming began, Tim Robbins and Derek Luke arrived to do their own research, and we got to know each other during the many script readings among the four of us. They were a joy to work with.

Filming began in September 2005 and took two months. Phillip Noyce was obsessed with the detail and the authenticity of the story, which drove me to delve deeper than I had expected to into my character's world. Many scenes were emotionally draining, and I'd have to sit in silence for hours afterwards to get a grip of my own world again. The work I did on that film stretched me like never before, and I grew from it.

During the shooting, Phillip told me that he truly believed

my medium was film, and he would do his bit to make sure the world got to witness my talent. This was huge praise indeed, and if this was a harbinger of things to come, I had plenty to look forward to. True to his word, he introduced me to Ruth Bornhauser, a young German talent manager based in LA, who was interested in managing my budding career. We spoke over the phone a couple of times, and I began to receive scripts for possible movie roles over the course of the next couple of years. Ruth also set to work to find me an agent in Los Angeles.

Sisanda, meanwhile, was loving his summer camp experience, although he found the kids challenging. His time there was now drawing to a close and in one of our long-distance conversations we settled on a wedding date.

I used Sisanda's absence to make overtures to my mother to rebuild our relationship and try to include her in the wedding preparations. Ever since our confrontation over my childhood issues, our conversations had been brief and icy, but through continuously forgiving her I had let go of my bitterness, and I hoped that the pride of seeing her daughter get married would bring relief to our strained relationship. She was certainly surprised that I was planning to marry, and was skeptical at our intention to wed so soon.

Sisanda returned at the end of September, after a three-month absence, and as soon as my mother met him, she was won over. On 17 December 2005 we said our marriage vows in a beautiful riverside ceremony in Port Alfred, surrounded by close friends and family. My mother was a very proud mother of the bride, and gave a speech at the reception. We kept the whole event very low profile to avoid media scrutiny.

That night, feeling secure and cherished in each other's waiting arms, we made sacred love to each other for the very first time. And so our lives together began.

The beginning of 2006 saw us working together on a series called *Hillside*, in which I played a thoracic surgeon and he the hospital's charming financial director. Working on the same set as husband and wife took some getting used to. We didn't quite know how to behave around each other when we got to work, and often had petty arguments about it. To my mind, working together was just an extension of our relationship at home. For Sisanda, our interaction as colleagues belonged in a completely different box. We'd be all chatty and lovey dovey as we left home, but the moment we got to work, I didn't exist. I'd ask him a question or want to sit with him during lunch, and he'd give me the cold shoulder. Then as soon as we left work, he'd cuddle up for a kiss. But by then I'd be sulking and not in the mood.

As time went on we figured it out, learning that we saw things differently and that our inner wiring was planets apart. So we agreed to meet each other halfway. Marriage was never simple or easy, I came to understand, but it was also a blessing, and a continuous course in problem-solving. Two people unite at the altar and vow to do life together, but it's when the celebrations end, I discovered, that the real work begins. For we bring to marriage our childhoods and all our beliefs and opinions about how life should be. Nobody had prepared me for this. But then building a harmonious life with someone you haven't lived with for most of your life is like starting from scratch; no one can ever prepare you for such a challenge.

When we weren't on set, we spent time doing charity work. I had already become a volunteer at Baby Haven, a Christian home for abandoned and orphaned infants up to one year old. The goal of Baby Haven was to care for the babies while trying to find them permanent homes. For a couple of hours a week I'd join volunteers from all walks of life to help feed, bath, dress and generally love the babies. It was heaven; I'd walk out beaming, my heart brimming with renewed life. Sometimes Sisanda couldn't resist the babies when he'd arrive to pick me up, and we'd end up spending an extra hour playing with them together. It was so fulfilling to step out of the comfort of our lives to empathise with others, giving of our skills and our time to bless and enrich their lives.

Later, we signed up together for a community project called Thisa Thuto, meaning 'strengthening education'. It focused on crime prevention through education and raising awareness of social issues through the arts, while cultivating dialogue among young people about their experiences with these issues. Over a two-month period, Sisanda and I ran a series of theatre workshops at twenty-five mostly disadvantaged schools in Alexandra and in the Free State. The idea was to help pupils prepare and stage a play involving music, dance and poetry, to highlight the issue of crime in their community and communicate that crime doesn't pay.

This was no easy task. Most schools we visited were plagued with poor infrastructure, staff absenteeism and demoralised pupils. But the kids were eager to learn from us. In a single day we'd visit four different schools and run a two-hour workshop at each. It was gruelling but immensely satisfying. We'd go home exhausted but elated from seeing young minds intrigued, inspired and awakened to their own natural talents and abilities. Sometimes we were mobbed on arrival by excited pupils who recognised us from television, and at one school in the Free State Sisanda ended with a deep cut beneath his eye, dangerously close to his eyeball.

As fulfilling as these experiences were, they were far from glamorous. Working with demoralised students and reluctant staff was like drawing blood from a stone, and some schools were so badly administered that it took up to an hour just to locate a teacher, find the pupils and get started, so we'd have to work our butts off to cram everything into the remaining hour. If we ran over time, we'd be late for the next one.

The only support we received was a stipend of R3000 a month and a list of schools. For the Free State trip, we were also given a hired car and accommodation at a guesthouse. We'd never been to many of the areas before, and had only a map and an address. Most of the roads were untarred and the streets in the tiny villages were often unmarked. But we never gave up.

We made a formidable team, Sisanda and I, and I'd do it all again in an instant. Every workshop was an amazing experience. The most memorable ones were always with the Grade One and Two pupils, who gave all of their little hearts to everything they did.

In September 2006, Sisanda and I left for a two-month American press tour for *Catch a Fire*, along with Tim Robbins and Derek Luke. Universal Pictures pulled out all the stops: first-class hotels, first-class flights, chauffeurs, plus a stylist with a brand-new wardrobe for my press appearances – including shoes and accessories – all of which I got to keep.

Our first stop was Toronto, where I watched the film for the first time. The audience gave it a standing ovation. During my make-up session that Sunday, Phillip rushed in excitedly with the *New York Times*. The entertainment section had a review of the year's best performances, titled *Scene Stealers: Six Breakthrough Performances of The Year*. At the top of the list was yours truly. 'Henna's Precious is uncommonly appealing; she has a grace and a freshness reminiscent of Audrey Hepburn,' it ran.

Among the many memorable compliments I received was

a comment in another publication that likened my arrival as a performer to the discovery of Nicole Kidman. The whole experience was one continuous, heady rush, and I felt like I'd become an overnight star.

We had screenings in at least ten different cities, each followed by a question-and-answer session and press interviews. In New York City, I was interviewed by as many as forty media representatives in one sitting. It was hard work, but I was happy as I returned to my hotel room, knowing that my Sisanda was there with me, because home was wherever he was.

My manager, Ruth, arranged to meet me in Washington DC, as we both happened to be going there at the same time. We'd spoken on the phone for almost a year now, and as I sat waiting for her in the plush lobby of The Ritz, it was hard to believe that this was our very first meeting; I felt like I'd known her forever. We got on like a shack on fire, and made plans to meet up again in LA when I arrived there in a couple of days.

The LA screening marked the official premiere of *Catch a Fire*, which I attended with Sisanda and Ruth. The pomp and excitement of the red carpet was completely overwhelming. At least twenty different voices were simultaneously calling my name and competing for my attention, while twenty cameras were flashing blindingly in my face like the lightning before a Jo'burg thunderstorm. Give me the work over the red-carpet drama any time, I thought. But I also understood that it was all a necessary part of showbiz, and that you couldn't have the biz without the buzz. It was important not to take it too seriously, and to keep focused on the main thing.

There I met Sheree of Paul Khoner, who remains my LA agent. Her role was to set up castings and negotiate contracts, while Ruth did the overall management and steering of my career. Everything was happening so fast and so effortlessly, it felt like my time had come and that God was running the schedule.

Those two months of touring the east and the west coasts were the most exciting, thrilling and adventurous season in my career. This was it for me, the big time. The doors stood wide open in front of me, and destiny and I were embraced in an enchanting dance. And what made it even sweeter was that I wasn't experiencing it alone.

Los Angeles was the final leg of our tour, and as our chauffeur drove us to the airport on the morning of our departure back home, we both had a strong feeling that our lives were about to change drastically. For me, however, the feeling was ominous, and on the flight back to South Africa I was plagued with nightmares.

Two weeks earlier, on our New York leg of the trip, I'd had an eerie premonition. Standing shoulder to shoulder with Sisanda on the packed subway back to Manhattan, a smile of deep satisfaction on my face, I had suddenly felt a gentle niggling in the depths of my soul. 'What if all of this were suddenly taken away?' it asked. 'Could you give it up, just for a while? Could you believe that if it's truly yours, it will return to you in a better way than you can imagine? Could you trust?'

I knew this presence. I'd sensed it before in all my moments of clarity. It was a peaceful, gentle, non-threatening presence, like a deep knowing. But I was afraid. We got off at our stop, and as we made our way to our room at the Waldorf Towers, I told Sisanda what had just happened. He was as surprised as me, but didn't say much.

What was going on? I took time out to be alone and prayed. 'God, if this is you, please give me the peace to let go of all this, to open my hand and trust you, knowing that you'd never dangle a carrot before me only to snatch it away as soon as I touch it. If this is you, I will trust that whatever you're about to do is for my own good, because you love me.' My prayer was a calm one of complete surrender, and I could sense God's reassuring presence.

What I didn't know was that deep inside, where it mattered most, I hadn't surrendered at all. I had no idea then that I was about to encounter one of the biggest battles of my life.

18

In Sickness and in Health

BACK IN SOUTH AFRICA AFTER the whirlwind and excitement of the trip, we quickly settled back into the administration of life. We had work to find and bills to pay. On the surface, all went smoothly. Our lives were interesting and successful, we were deeply in love, and there were plenty of good times. But despite the happy picture, something else was brewing beneath the surface. Only we couldn't quite put a finger on it.

There's a certain level of safety in the distance of dating, where aspects of you and your partner lie hidden. You have the luxury of space and time to prepare yourself and be on your best behaviour, to put your best foot forward. You can keep your carelessness for when you're behind closed doors, not attempting to impress anyone. You can choose what part of yourself to expose and what to expose yourself to. It's like putting on a pair of tight stilettos for an appointment, bearing the pain, comforted by the knowledge that in a few hours you'll be able to kick them off again and let your toes breathe.

But in a marriage there's no such luxury. The distance and space disappear, and spouses suddenly get a front-row seat in the drama of each other's lives.

Within a year of our marriage, both my husband and I began to realise that something was wrong. We had no idea of its source, but I believed it lay with me. It had begun to reveal itself as soon as we crossed the threshold into married life. We never talked about it, because we'd never identified it; it was the proverbial elephant in the room.

There were long, cold silences in the mornings. As the first signs of daylight crept through our window panes, I'd pull the covers over my head so the day couldn't find me; it was my daily ritual of hide and seek. From the moment of opening my eyes, hopelessness greeted me, draining my body of all energy or enthusiasm. We were newly married, supposedly in the honeymoon phase, yet I had no energy for anything, not for getting up, sex, eating or even – perhaps especially – talking to my husband.

I was constantly trying to hide from my husband. It didn't happen consciously; it was a habit I'd come into the marriage with, a survival mechanism. I made no attempt to reveal to him all the baggage I'd accumulated – I'd grown so accustomed to carrying it, I was hardly aware of its weight. To explain my strange behaviour, lack of libido and constant fatigue, I had to come up with a myriad excuses. Sometimes

I was so tired that getting off the couch to give him a hug when he got home felt like a four-kilometre hike. He'd be standing there reaching for a hug and I'd say, 'I'm tired love, really tired,' and he'd stand there paralysed in puzzlement. He took it as rejection, as me withholding affection because I didn't care.

Although my symptoms couldn't be explained by my hormonal cycle, there was nothing obvious to alert my husband to something more sinister at play; he just thought me odd. After all, he'd been attracted by my quirky personality and non-conformity. But my withholding of affection and my unpredictable, irrational rages were certainly hurting him. Later, when we knew what the source of the problem had been, he told me, 'Honey, I just began to accept that you were an unhappy person and that I would be in an unhappy marriage.' It probably wouldn't have been sustainable, but he loved me that much.

My interpersonal skills were just as shot as my nerves. Replying to messages, emails and phone calls had never come easily to me, but now even the thought of returning a call overwhelmed me. If I was asked why I hadn't, I felt backed into a corner, and reacted like a deer caught in headlights. I even found driving overwhelming, and often begged my husband to drive me around. Seemingly effortless tasks, like applying for a phone line, could easily drive me to tears. I was like a thin, dry twig, constantly on the verge of snapping. Sisanda was more than kind and patient. He handled all the admin it took to run our lives and become increasingly protective of me; it became tough to convince him that I could handle anything on my own.

Behind my indifferent, aloof, this-bitch-bites exterior, those who got to know me picked up my fragility. But inside my marriage, I was now tottering on the verge of shattering.

We'd be on our way to visit friends or attend a function and my stomach would be tied up in knots as I imagined all the negative perceptions people might have of my appearance or my conversation, so compromised was my self-image. I'd sometimes suffer a last-minute anxiety attack so intense that I wouldn't be able to go.

Unanticipated changes of plan completely tipped the apple cart and threw me into a fever of emotion; I had no capacity to adapt on the spur of the moment. My reactions were always extreme, either calmly indifferent or highly neurotic. I became a hypochondriac. I feared every germ, virus or disease, and the slightest pain in one of my breasts would trigger a frenzy of speculation about breast cancer.

As disconcerting as all this was for others, for me the suffering was intense, and this constant tumult left me drained of energy for anything worthwhile. I was unhappy, agitated, anxious and terrified of just about everything. Anything could push me over the edge of reason, and my reaction was often disproportionate to the weight of the issue. Our first home together, in a beautiful, tree-lined complex in Sandton, was on the fourth floor. Whenever I saw more than one person in the lift, I'd hang back and wait for an empty one, such were my space issues and my fear of people. I hadn't shaken my childhood distrust of adults; if anything, it had grown. So I hid from the world.

Absurdly, I actually believed I was keeping my inner turmoil hidden from my husband, such was the severity of my self-delusion. I didn't even know what it was I was hiding, yet I was determined to hide it. I felt like a fugitive in my own body, always on the verge of losing my mind. It was a constant struggle to see hope in any situation, so overwhelmed was I by every negative emotion I experienced. I was deeply troubled and burdened by something I couldn't see, and slowly losing my will to live.

I did begin to suspect that I might be depressed, but I didn't know where to begin to tackle such an issue. My cultural disposition and world view couldn't allow this train of thought. I'd never known a black person who was depressed. My cultural legacy demanded that I stop feeling sorry for myself; things were far worse for most black Africans, and I didn't have to look far for proof. Black people didn't sit around bemoaning their misfortune; they were professional sufferers, and just kept doing what they had to do. Clearly, my schooling among white kids had made me too soft. I needed to snap out of this and just get on with life, and that was what I kept trying do. Yet day by day I was unravelling, and the more I isolated myself, the more my seams strained under the mounting pressure.

At times I feared completely losing my mind and going crazy, like the barefoot, dishevelled lunatic from my Pimville neighbourhood, who endlessly walked every street in Soweto, from one end to the other, talking to himself and defecating in his pants. That's where I was headed if I didn't get a grip. I had to maintain more control, exercise more, pray more, read more and *stay calm*.

I was constantly restless and irritable, as if an invisible hand was poking me from behind and winding me up. I couldn't take stillness and calm; it was sheer torment. I wanted every moment to be speeded up. And everyone else was to blame for my raging inferno. The smallest oversight by my husband would set me off. I'd blame him for my every mood, unaware that he was just a scapegoat. I saw his frustration, not knowing how to reach out to me, and it hurt me to see what I was putting him through. I was in a dark pit, refusing to call for help, for fear that he'd decide it was all too much and walk away.

To me our marriage had represented a safe place where I could rest and hide from the big bad world. But suspecting that I was sick shattered the picture-perfect world I'd imagined our marriage to be. I was terrified that Sisanda would label me crazy and a psycho. I became a hostage to the fear that he would soon realise he'd made a grave mistake in marrying a mentally ill woman, and would probably opt out before he embarrassed or endangered himself. After all, this wasn't what he'd signed up for. So I hid from him. And in the self-imposed silence, my wound festered.

For Sisanda and me it was a hard road. My husband prayed for me every day; we prayed continuously for our marriage and its survival. The patience with which my husband peeled away at the layers that shielded my heart was gentle and persistent. But the more exposed and vulnerable I became, the more I tried to hide. In the middle of my fits of rage, he would say in the softest voice, 'What can I do to fix this, honey? I'm on your side; I'm not going anywhere.'

'Nothing!' I'd scream at him. 'There's nothing you can do!'

I didn't mean any of it; I'd been in this prison for so long, I feared that trying to escape would be worse than staying in. I had found a way to live and survive in the chaos. Here I was being offered first aid and a healing salve, yet I feared it because even in recovery I knew there would be more pain.

Every day we danced the dance of the broken horse and the horse whisperer. But no matter how much I pushed him away, he refused to give in. Sisanda had come for my heart and he wasn't going anywhere till he had it. I was wild with pain yet intoxicated by the drama and determined never to give in. But my whisperer was unflinching and determined to conquer. He read my silences, sat out the hours of dripping pain, and all it took was the slightest glimpse of recovery to rekindle his hope.

I would often marvel at the love that drove this man, at his selflessness, patience and unrelenting pursuit of this woman who I no longer recognised as myself. All fingers pointed to God. I'd only heard of such profound love in the context of God, a love as jealous and demanding as the grave, a love waters couldn't quench. The Bible said that God himself was love, that there was no greater love than to lay down one's life for a friend, and now I was watching it play out right in front of me. The more Sisanda prayed for God to heal me and rescue me from my torment, the more God seemed to answer by filling him with his own love to cover my nakedness, and the patience to wade through it all. I watched it grow every day; it was nothing short of a miracle.

Every day, hour, minute and heartbeat, Sisanda lay down his life for me. I wanted to be deserving of his love, to be found worthy of it, and it angered me that I couldn't. Shame and pride got in the way of receiving this unmerited grace. Was this not the great love I'd dreamt of my whole life, offering itself to me without reserve? But where I'd come from, there was no undeserved or unconditional love. And no effort to be deserving had brought me the love I craved, either.

But, of course, there were also many good moments when we had great sex and laughed really hard. And we were good friends, which helped. Our sexless courtship had created an opportunity to get to know each other without the complications that a physical relationship brings, enough for us to have been convinced that we could spend forever together. And most of our hurdles weren't uncommon for people in their first year of marriage.

Fortunately, my acting work also brought some order to my world. When I was on set giving wings to people's stories, deciphering their emotional landscapes and translating them for the audience, I was most at peace. This was where I felt God's complete affirmation and pleasure. Here I was free, even of my own perceived limitations. My work was my prayer, my worship and a steady grip on the spinning turntable of my life. Yet even there, my restlessness and brittleness were starting to show and cause waves.

19

To Live in LA

OUR INTERNATIONAL TRIP to promote *Catch a Fire* had changed something in us; it awakened us to the possibility of what our lives could become beyond the boundaries of the world we'd always known. There was a whole world to be discovered. We'd taken a bite and the taste now lingered. We wanted more.

We'd always seen ourselves as citizens of the world. I believe that's one of the things that attracted us to one another; an appetite for the extraordinary that beckoned in each other's eyes. We were dreamers, and instead of calming the hunger for adventure in the other, we fuelled each other's wanderlust.

Our Morningside flat was beautiful, but the sterility of

the northern suburbs was anaesthetising us, narrowing our scope. We had begun obsessing about security and whether our car windows were sufficiently smash-proof. We longed for a more in-your-face, raw and gritty environment to inspire our creativity. We wanted to get out of our comfort zone and back to the cutting edge, to encounter the real South Africa and become part of the solution. So we popped over to see the new downtown developments where derelict buildings were being refurbished into Manhattan-style loft apartments to entice people back to city living.

We settled on a funky loft on Quinn Street in the cultural precinct, and set about getting a bank loan. I wasn't too hopeful, since banks aren't eager to give loans to people in our profession. We did eventually get one, and I'd often joke to Sisanda that they didn't actually realise they'd just given us a loan.

Around May that year I was offered a role in *Soul City*, a popular and longstanding TV series on SABC1, aimed at educating South Africans about health and social issues, living positively and dealing with problems. It was a successful attempt at community development and nation building through storytelling. I believed in *Soul City* and its mission and felt the story was important and needed to be told. In tandem with finding God, getting married and starting charity work, I was experiencing a new search for meaning in life, something beyond the superficial partying and glamour that came with celebrity. Just as my interest in social issues was developing, I was being offered a role that embodied this. Life and art were in harmony once again.

Since my spiritual conversion, I had stopped drinking and smoking and adopted healthier lifestyle choices, which helped a bit to reduce the pressure inside me. Yet a fire was still burning inside me; I had an insatiable hunger for meaning and purpose, to be a part of something that would affect the generations who came after me. I wanted the world around me to be different because I'd been in it.

The result was an increasing intolerance of injustice, which I no longer felt able to overlook. One morning, after our pay had been delayed for over a month, I refused to return to work without proof of payment. Since I was playing the lead, it forced production to do something about it. The whole cast and crew were grateful I'd put my foot down, because everyone benefited. In another instance, I refused to work until the extras were fed. Grannies, mothers and their babies would be called onto set at six o'clock in the morning – often without breakfast – and while the actors got breakfast and mid-morning snacks, the extras were expected to go without any sustenance until lunch time. Child labour laws were being violated at every turn, and I just couldn't ignore it any more. What was the point of being the lead with everything at my beck and call, I wondered, if I wasn't prepared to use this power to help others around me? I began to check what time the babies and their mothers had arrived, and I'd kick up a fuss if they were kept on set too long. I also made it my business to find out if mothers had filled in the necessary paperwork, to ensure they got paid before they left for the day.

These acts of protest got me into trouble with my agent, and crew members and production began accusing me once again of being a prima donna. I didn't care, because this time it was for a good cause.

I was also hungry to advance my career. Although I'd done well locally, and was often among the first choices for many local television and film roles, it felt time for the next step. My achievements in the South African entertainment industry were something to be proud of, but if I was really any good, I felt my skills had to be tested against the best in the world. I could remain a big fish in a small pond or I could swim out to sea and battle it out with the big fish until I grew big enough to hold my own. That was my plan. I felt a need to reach for more. My capacity to carry more responsibility had grown, together with the weariness of fighting the same old battles, trying to convince production companies that actors deserved more than to be tacked onto the budget as an afterthought. Fighting for remuneration to match the weight of your work was considered big-headed. I'd grown disillusioned with our local industry and ready for fresh challenges.

All these factors were agitating me, challenging me to do something more. But there was also something else at play: an increasing restlessness, a driving urge that if I didn't get out of where I was immediately, I would die; a desperation for something I couldn't name; an overarching anxiety that sharpened every sensation, making me rough around the edges, sharp and cutting with my words, impatient with the world and even more so with myself.

I was hard on people. I'd become critical and hard to please. Nothing – including my marriage, my career and my body – quite measured up to my expectations. I had an insatiable desire for perfection and sought it at every turn. But the more I sought it, the less my life measured up. It was driving me crazy.

Although I still enjoyed my work, I was struggling to keep my emotions under control on set. In my self-criticism, I could never let up, relax or go easy on myself. Drama seemed to follow me. I was difficult to work with because I spoke my mind without a second thought. I often had a valid point, but my methods weren't always constructive, especially in such a volatile, high-pressure industry where emotions often ran high.

Rumours of what had taken place on set often got exaggerated as they spread through the grapevine, and I got painted as a kind of Cruella De Vil. In one incident in February 2006, soon after our marriage, when we were both in the cast of *Hillside*, we were shooting crazy hours in a real hospital on a shoestring budget. Among the appalling treatment of the cast and crew was the requirement that we all share a single dressing room – men and women, young and old, lead and extras, lock, stock and barrel. We got on with it anyway, because most of us had caught the vision of the producers and understood that they were trying to pull rabbits out of hats with the little they had.

At around eleven o'clock one night, Grant, the director, asked me to perform a stunt differently from the way it was written in the script. The directions called for me to trip and fall out of frame, but he wanted the camera to follow me down and catch me hitting the ground. I wasn't willing to perform something that dangerous without a stunt coordinator to direct me safely through it, as was the norm on all previous sets I'd been on, and I calmly told him this. Annoyed, he called for a mattress, and proceeded to demonstrate how I should do it.

'See, it's easy!' he insisted. 'Even I can do it!'

But I well knew that if I injured myself in any way, the production would take no responsibility. So again, I told him calmly that I wouldn't do it.

He blew his fuse in front of everyone present. 'You stupid bitch!' he yelled. 'Who the fuck do you think you are?' As he ranted on, I became still calmer, turned around and walked off set.

The next morning I called my agent, Penny, and explained what had happened. I added that I refused to work with him for the remainder of the production. Penny felt I was well

145

within my rights. After liaising with the production heads, who apologised on his behalf and ordered him to apologise, Penny called back to say it had all been sorted out. I never saw Grant again, but the version that spread through the industry was that I was such a prima donna I'd got poor nice-guy Grant fired for no reason.

I was growing increasingly frustrated with the way actors were treated in our industry, and I'd worked on enough international productions to know that it was well below acceptable norms. I wanted out and away from it all.

During discussions with my agent, we decided that it was best to strike while the iron was hot, and take advantage of the excitement *Catch a Fire* had generated internationally. The best way was for me to move to Los Angeles, where my presence would greatly assist my manager and agent to increase awareness of my abilities. Being in South Africa was also slowing down the casting process, and the admin involved had grown quite tedious. When Ruth sent me a script, Sisanda and I would then have to shoot the audition ourselves and upload it via email to Ruth, a process that usually took up to a week.

I certainly pushed for the move more than Sisanda did. I felt stressed out and trapped, destined to face the same old battles. Sisanda wanted more time to think it over. Two years earlier he'd been ready to move to LA to study at USC, but that dream had been shelved, and now I was asking him to dust it off again. Now, though, he had a greater sense of responsibility, and he wanted to know he had a plan to look after his family, despite all the drama I imposed. Sisanda was the cautious one, but the restlessness inside me couldn't wait; it was do or die. I didn't need a proper plan of action; the dream was enough to feed and shelter me. Ultimately Sisanda was supportive of my dream and willing to help me do whatever it took to further my career. He fully understood what it meant to have an agent and a manager raring to go, and they'd also made it clear that getting my career off the ground in another country would take time and needed me there. So we agreed that I shouldn't miss this opportunity. While I pursued my acting career, Sisanda would find ways to move towards producing and directing, something he'd wanted to do for some time.

In late August 2007 we made the decision to move permanently to Los Angeles. I had accepted an invitation to participate in a film festival in Ireland, so I already had a paid ticket as far as Europe in three weeks' time. It seemed too good an opportunity to miss. But that meant we had just three short weeks to get our move organised.

As the gravity of our decision sank in, there was so much to think about that I was sometimes overwhelmed to the point of total paralysis. I relied heavily on my friends, my sister Koketso, and my mom for strength at this time. By now my relationship with my mother was calmer and more civil; I was now a full-grown woman and wife, and if a conversation took a turn I didn't like, I could always hand over to Sisanda, who acted as a buffer when interactions threatened to become too emotional.

We hardly slept, as every day was jam-packed with the administration of leaving. We sold our car, found a tenant to rent our flat fully furnished, and put all our valuables and sentimental belongings in a friend's storage facility. The days leading up to our departure were strained with anxiety and sadness at the thought of leaving behind our friends and family.

Friends organised a surprise farewell dinner. The biggest surprise was hearing during their tear-jerking speeches how much we meant to our friends and what an inspiration our marriage was to many. People truly wished us well, and showed genuine admiration for our courage. Many also came to the airport to say goodbye. I still have a clear picture of them and some family members waving us goodbye, fighting back tears as we blew kisses from the boarding gate. Then we trudged off, hand in hand, ready to take on whatever lay ahead and thankful to have each other.

We left in mid-September 2007. Our first stop was the four-day film festival in Ireland where *Catch a Fire* would be screened, and I was to give a talk and facilitate acting workshops. We travelled via London, and running around the huge airport carrying the maximum luggage allowance was no fun. But the festival organisers were paying me a stipend of US$125 a day on top of food, transport and accommodation, and had provided a return flight to South Africa, which we kept open-ended, just in case we might need it.

When the film festival ended, we spent a night in a quaint hotel in Dublin. Sisa and I stayed up most of the night, cruising the Internet for cheap flights from London to LA. All the money we had lay strewn over the bed as we counted out every penny, separating the different currencies, which included rands, euros, pounds and even some left-over dollars from our US trip the year before. We finally found flights for $900 for the two of us.

This time there would be no chauffeur-driven Lincolns and SUVs, and no fancy hotels, stylists or make-up artists. We were roughing it, and we knew it wouldn't be a walk in the park. But we looked forward to the adventure. There was no turning back now. To join the big league in LA was every performer's dream, and now the opportunity had presented itself. I was convinced that when chance made an appearance you simply had to grab it, so that when it left you, as it inevitably would, you weren't left standing where it found you.

By the time we reached LA I had a bad case of flu. I knew my illness was my body's reaction to the stress and emotional roller coaster leading up to our departure. It was the price of living fast and furious, and my body was vehemently objecting. My nose and chest were congested, and I'd over-medicated myself to numb the aches in my body. We exchanged the rest of our rands for dollars, as by now we'd already spent those we had on food and medication.

The evening air was warm and humid as we stepped out of the terminal. The buses had long retired for the day, so we had to take a cab. I felt like death, and was greatly relieved to finally be seated again as the cab drove us to our destination – Phillip Noyce's apartment on Melrose Boulevard in West Hollywood.

The sermon playing in the car was soothing and reassuring, and made me feel that everything would be okay. As we drove along Highway 101, with the city lights sweeping past like shooting stars, I felt exhilarated. I had dived off the edge, into the unknown.

Besides Phillip, the only people expecting us were God, my manager Ruth and my agent Sheree. The pastor of the LA congregation had also been alerted by the pastor of our church to be on the lookout for us, and to our surprise, he called us the following day to invite us to an impromptu meeting at the church the following night.

Phillip had asked his PA, Meredith, to wait at the office, which was next to his apartment, to hand over the keys. It was good to see her, but as we chatted I could hardly keep my eyes open, so I excused myself and went upstairs, where I passed out without unpacking. I didn't feel much better the next morning, but Ruth came over that evening bringing

some good Chinese food – with copious amounts of ginger
in mine to fight the flu. As I lay on the couch, Ruth took us
through the details of my first audition. She also warned
of the looming Hollywood writers' strike, which, if it went
ahead, would be bad for my prospects. But she didn't think
it would last long. I drifted in and out of the conversation
as Ruth and Sisanda began to discuss our urgent meeting
with the highly acclaimed South African emigration lawyer,
Chris Wright, who would help us apply for work permits
and our much-coveted Green Cards.

Phillip generously gave us full use of his phone and
Internet, as well as his Lexus, which we used sparingly
to avoid spending too much on gas, and concentrated on
figuring out the bus system. Sisanda took responsibility for
the transport arrangements. 'Don't worry about anything
but your audition. I'll take care of the rest.' I couldn't have
managed without him. If ever I felt like God was playing
hide and seek with me, I only had to look at Sisa to remind
myself that God was indeed by my side; Sisanda was my
living sign.

The writers' strike began two days after our arrival,
while I was still sick with flu. This meant that not many
new projects or opportunities would be available. But Ruth
focused on the bright side: we'd be able to get one-on-one
meetings with casting directors at the big studios.

Now that we'd finally arrived, I felt we were exactly where
we needed to be. Los Angeles presented a very different
reality to the one we were used to, and sometimes it was like
being in a movie ourselves. LA was unashamedly superficial
and bent over backwards for anyone who was famous,
rich and white. And for all its glorious reputation as the
entertainment capital of the world, it was a surprisingly dull,
soulless place, almost like a haunted town. Its inhabitants

were like ghosts of their former selves, its buildings were bland and uninspiring, and the atmosphere was kind of eerie, like something out of the movie *Baghdad Café*.

My first audition, for a film called *The Justice League of America*, took place during our second week. I was really looking forward to it, but as I entered the casting director's office and introduced myself to the two young girls behind the desk, neither looked up. Without once glancing at me, one of them managed to tell me where to sit and which forms to fill in. I reminded myself that I wasn't there to make friends. There was no queue, so I did my audition right away and left. Sisanda was waiting for me at a corner shop, and I was very glad he was the first person I saw after that. I never heard back from my agent about it.

When Phillip sprung a surprise on us, suddenly needing the apartment for his nephew, we hastily moved in with a family we'd met at church when we were in LA the year before. After hearing our predicament, they generously invited us to stay with them indefinitely.

The Johnsons were a solid, hardworking black American family with four children, Nathan, Rayna, Brendan and Rachel. The children were polite with a maturity that belied their age. Their house in Reseda had three bedrooms, and the girls gave us their room, while one went to sleep on the couch and the other in her parents' room. We were bowled over by their kindness, but naturally self-conscious and hypersensitive to everyone's needs, always unsure if we were stepping on anyone's toes. Never good at asking for or receiving help, I felt rather stretched, but at the same time extremely grateful. We still had enough money for food and other personal needs, but the Johnsons always insisted we eat with them.

My second audition was for the role of the Jamaican mother

in *Notorious*, the life story of hip hop star Notorious B.I.G. His mother's accent was a mix of American and Jamaican, since she had come to America in her teens. My look suited the role, which meant I wouldn't need hair extensions – known as a weave – which I refused to adopt. Americans always assumed that I didn't have a weave because I was a primitive African, not because I didn't want one.

We had to catch two buses to reach the audition venue at Fox Studios, and then spent a good fifteen minutes running around, freaking out because we were late, trying to find the right building in the huge and confusing Fox complex. But the adrenalin rush helped overcome my nerves. When we finally arrived, the casting director, an extroverted black American woman named Twinkie, seemed genuinely intrigued that I was African, and kept giggling at my ballet posture, turned out feet and 'proper' manner.

The audition went really well, and I was called back for a second and a third one, which the director attended. On our way home after the third audition, Ruth called to say that the director was blown away. He'd told her that the last time he saw work of this calibre was when he watched Sydney Poitier. It was between me and Angela Bassett now, but it was likely they'd go with Angela, who was a more recognised name in American cinema, which would give it a boost at the box office. It wasn't the news I was hoping to hear, but I could accept losing to an actress of that calibre.

In the meantime, we met with Chris Wright, the immigration lawyer, who explained that it would cost $7000 (R35 000) to apply for a Green Card, with half due upfront and the rest after three months. It would take at least a year to be processed, but we'd receive a work permit in about two months. On the bus home we considered our chances of raising the money, which weren't good. Time wasn't on our side. Despite our ten-year visitor's visas, without work permits we couldn't stay longer than six months at a stretch. To get our paperwork sorted we needed $3500 immediately, or employers who were willing to apply for work permits on our behalf – but first they'd need to prove that they couldn't find an American to do the job. We agreed that working illegally wasn't an option, believing that we needed to honour the law of the land to be honoured in return, and that living like fugitives – or getting deported – didn't appeal, even to an adventurous twosome like ourselves.

Being turned out of Phillip's flat turned out to have been a blessing. The Johnsons offered a stable family environment that kept us grounded and fended off our loneliness in the midst of all the challenges facing us. It also helped keep us focused on what was important, like our marriage. As the external pressures mounted, we took everything too personally and argued continually, although here we had to keep our voices hushed or wait till we were out to have a full go.

We so badly wanted this whole thing to work, but it was looking increasingly impossible and our backs were against the wall. Sisa sent out his resumé to many different companies, and got his first job interview at the end of October at a firm called The Company Productions. It all went well until the interviewer realised how much work hiring a foreigner would entail.

In the meantime, James Johnson asked us to give his children acting lessons, for which he offered to pay us. We couldn't accept the money, but giving the children lessons was a treat and gave me something to look forward to. I spent time gathering resources and compiling lessons, which kept my mind off our worries, and gave me a chance to brush up on technique and refresh my skills. The kids loved it as much as I did. They were all being home schooled, making it easy to slot in an acting lesson once a week, and Rachel, the youngest, showed a natural flair.

Church was a regular part of our week. In addition to the Sunday-morning service, we attended a Wednesday-night cell meeting at members' homes in Studio City, where we met new people, made new friends, shared our frustrations and received support through prayer. The members found our story fascinating; some were actors themselves, so they could relate to our issues, which comforted us and helped us realise that our problems weren't unique. The industry was tough for everyone there, and they couldn't fathom why we'd left behind the favour and position we enjoyed in the industry back home to brave the uncertainty of Hollywood. They thought we were daring and brave, and drew inspiration from us, while we gained a healthy new perspective in return.

I often thought about my family and missed them. I worried about my sister who was writing her matric now, and I missed my brother too. And with the objectivity of distance, I realised just how much I loved my mother, what an amazing woman she was, and how much she'd sacrificed to make things work. When I heard the song 'Mama' by Boyz II Men on the radio one day, I cried like a baby. I also thought about Africa, and what an intrinsic part of me it was. No matter how far I travelled, I carried Africa in my bosom.

I felt a mounting conflict inside me. With all my safety nets dismantled and nothing familiar here to hold on to, I felt stripped and bare, without a fig leaf to conceal my tender parts. Even my closest friends seemed to have forgotten me. I'd send lengthy emails and wait weeks to receive a few lines in return. Those who'd promised to keep in touch were the most silent.

Here in LA I was having to fight to be acknowledged and given a chance. I felt like I was lost in the middle of a bridge, hesitant to move forward and terrified of going back. But without my usual crutches to lean on, my hands were free to hold onto God. I prayed incessantly, sometimes just to get through the day. I spoke to him about everything, from the smallest to the greatest. My focus was on keeping mentally strong. I said my affirmations and went running every morning. I couldn't let my mind slip; I had to hold on to the faith that there was a purpose in all this, that something would give. I just had to make sure that it wasn't me.

The writers' strike was still going full steam, so new scripts weren't being written and the industry had almost ground to a halt. If anyone had underestimated the power that the writing community wielded, they were now eating humble pie. I often saw pickets outside the studios on my way in for meetings. But Ruth was doing a good job getting me an audience with some of the most prolific casting directors in Hollywood. When she mentioned that I was in town they were eager to meet me, as most of them had seen *Catch a Fire*. I was getting a truly encouraging response, but the timing was unfortunate, and this was compounded by not having a weave, a fairer skin or an American accent.

Black women in America were obsessed with fair skin, not only in the industry but at schools as well. Most were using skin-lightening products, and some even took pills to make their skins whiter. They'd been brainwashed into believing that the closer to Caucasian their features leaned, the more beautiful they were and the more likely to succeed. To me this was a foreign concept, and I found it heart-breaking that so many had been bamboozled into believing this. I was becoming increasingly grateful to be African – we'd put those demons behind us. I certainly wasn't prepared to try to look whiter in order to get more work. If that was what it took to make it here, I was happy to walk away. Changing my look and appearance to portray a character was fine with me, but I refused to give up my identity to get work.

Every actress who was serious about working in LA had to master the accent, but I could accept having to learn an American accent, because it wasn't tied to race, nationality or origin, but to the roles on offer. Mine was coming along nicely, I felt, although it would have done better under less pressured circumstances. I'd bought a Standard American Accent teaching CD from an acting resource store in Studio City, and downloaded it onto my iPod. I practised in the mornings while I was jogging. I also tried to practise it in conversation, but I'd regress whenever I spoke to anyone from home – annoyingly, they'd give me grief about my phony new accent. Yet developing it was essential because I was auditioning for American roles, and I also needed a deeper grasp of their mannerisms and way of doing things.

Black casting directors were the most discouraging. Everything about me was wrong; they'd constantly point out that I spoke too well and was far too 'proper' or polished, and would struggle to convince audiences that I was from the ghetto. I got far more kindness and support from white casting directors, and soon I began asking Ruth before each meeting if the person I'd be seeing was black or white. This would greatly influence my mood.

Going to castings was always a positive step, but Sisa and I would often argue on the way there, and I'd arrive at the casting feeling drained. Sometimes we'd catch the wrong bus or underestimate the walking time from our stop to the location, and our eyes were forever glued to a giant street map that we never left home without. It felt like a never-ending episode of *The Amazing Race*, complete with crying fits and arguments, except that ours wasn't a show – this was for real.

On the home front things were peaceful. Returning to the oasis of the Johnson residence after a hard day's digging for treasure in unyielding Hollywood ground was comforting. Raelynne, James's wife, was an intelligent, regal, soft-spoken woman ready to nurture anyone who came into her home. I'd spend late nights chatting to her on the couch, her reassuring voice affirming my identity and supporting me at the most unexpected times. We shared many meaningful moments that filled the cracks in my soul. At times she would randomly walk up to me with a big smile, kiss me on the cheek and wrap me in a warm, loving hug, like she knew I needed it just then.

The mystery of God's hand was apparent to us in their household. We were both learning so much about how to be parents, discipline children lovingly and foster a peaceful, loving home environment. It was like being in the front row watching *Happy Homes for Dummies*. We took in a great deal without realising it, and later we'd compare notes on what we'd learnt. Both of us knew we were meant to have stayed here with this family, because neither of us had ever witnessed the harmony we saw modelled here.

Another audition came up, and Ruth and I argued about whether I should go. It was an Ice Cube film about a talented twelve-year-old who was the only girl in the football team. I was to read for the mother role, a hardworking single mom from the ghetto. I'd seen these Ice Cube family movies. They weren't my favourite genre and I still wasn't comfortable going for 'typical black American' roles. But Ruth stressed that it would be a good opportunity to be seen by the casting director, who might remember me for a future role in something else. So, begrudgingly, I went. Time wasn't on my side, and I also wanted Ruth to know that I respected her opinion. I greatly valued my relationship with Ruth, her belief in me, and her hard work and constant pushing to try to open up doors.

But it was tough to portray a character I didn't believe in or understand. Every performer knows that feeling when you connect with the soul of a role or a character, when every part of you wants to pour life and meaning into their every thought, word and emotion. I'd learnt to trust that inner voice when choosing my roles, and I'd been right every time. Yet I went to the audition anyway, catching two buses and walking another three kilometres to the casting venue, while my make-up melted in the sweltering California heat. Once again I was thanked for being professional, knowing my lines and not needing to read from the script, something I was always very particular about. Casting directors in LA found me unusual and were generally intrigued by me as well as by my interpretations of the roles I auditioned for. At times I enjoyed this, but sometimes it made me extremely self-conscious.

The actors and actresses I met at church and social gatherings pointed out how fortunate I was to make it to the movie castings I did. Access was based on your current body of work, and many performers who'd been in LA for over ten years still couldn't get a manager or an agent to even see them, let alone take them on. I was auditioning for work that only the top ten per cent of actors could audition for. This was encouraging, but from my vantage point, things weren't looking good. When I tried out for *Fast and Furious III*, Ruth got feedback that they were very impressed with my audition, but had decided to go with a girl of a different race. I felt I'd have stood a better chance if I had a long weave and skimpier clothing.

A few days into November, South African friends of ours who'd moved to LA two years before us invited us out to supper. We'd been in touch with Sunu and Rene since we arrived, but hadn't yet found an opportunity to connect. At dinner in Santa Monica that night they were very supportive, and invited us to come and stay with them for a while. I was eager to take up their offer, fearing that we might have overstayed our welcome at the Johnsons. Sisanda insisted we hadn't, but it seemed prudent to move out before we got on their nerves. So we moved in with the Goneras and their two adorable children, Josh and Hannah. The Goneras were a lively bunch and full of creativity. Rene was a dancer and also very skilled in design and interior decorating, while Sunu worked as a director in Hollywood. We'd met through the industry back home. Sunu and Sisanda had been friends before our marriage, and I'd met Sunu during a casting for a commercial he was directing.

Dinner-table conversations with them were always vibrant and filled with laughter. Through them we got to know a dear friend of theirs, a lovely young Zimbabwean woman called Rita Mbanga, who'd grown up in Cape Town. Her father had recently bought her a new car, and she generously offered us the use of her old car, a nippy little Ford Escort. We were touched by her readiness to entrust it to us, especially since she'd barely met us. When we realised we couldn't afford the compulsory $80 a month for insurance, the Goneras offered to pay it until we were financially stable enough to cover it.

The car was a treat. It was far quicker to get to auditions and meetings, and we didn't get as lost because we could navigate from Google maps, though I still preferred Sisanda to drive me, as I didn't adapt well to driving on the right. The car also meant we could go on weekly date nights or spend afternoons at the Farmers' Market, which we loved, and long strolls along Santa Monica Boulevard were also a favourite.

We celebrated Thanksgiving with the Johnsons and their extended family. It felt like something out of a *Big Momma* movie; the children's maternal grandmother spoke in a fast, singsong, Baptist-choir voice, and she was kind, wise and funny. Thanksgiving was about eating as much as you could, and when you thought you couldn't eat any more, you had to make some room for sweet potato pie, pumpkin pie and peach cobbler. Consumption levels bordered on sinful.

Table talk all over America was centred on the presidential race, and the upcoming election was definitely the most talked about in American history, with Republicans and Democrats getting into heated arguments. We favoured Barack Obama, and were closely following the debates and polls prior to the primaries. I even read his *Audacity of Hope* to get some insight into the man who'd given new meaning to the phrase 'Yes we can'. America was pregnant with hope, and in some ways it gave strength to our own wavering light.

An atmosphere of possibility and optimism prevailed in America, not unlike South Africa in 1994 before our first democratic elections. Despite our own personal drama, it was a deeply moving time to be in America, and it was thrilling to engage in debates about the different electoral candidates. But Americans take their politics very personally, and our cell-group leader had felt the need to rule that politics not be discussed at cell meetings, as conversations often got so heated, people could end up losing their salvation over differing views.

Our money supply was dire. We were reliant on funds generated from our assets back home, which wasn't much after we'd paid the monthly bills we were still liable for, some of which were in arrears. All our hopes hinged on raising enough money to pay the deposit on our Green Card application.

Sisanda was still sending his resumé out, but nothing had turned up so far. Meanwhile, I continued going to castings. In November I auditioned for a role in a pilot called *Revolution*. It was always funny spotting so many actors and actresses I recognised from TV shows and movies filling in the same forms and waiting in the same room as me. Pilot season was now in full force, but with the writers still on strike, the usual influx of work it represented was significantly diminished.

Soon we were on the lookout for another place to stay. Rene and I were getting into arguments and generally stepping on one another's toes. She'd gotten really mad when I didn't lock the front door one day while I was making lunch for the kids. Coming from South Africa, she was neurotic about security. I thought it best that we move before our friendship deteriorated any further.

We began praying for a solution, and a week before Christmas we received two offers of accommodation. One was from the South African Consulate General, whom we'd called to say hello to, after becoming acquainted the previous year when she'd hosted the *Catch a Fire* group for a lunch. She was excited to hear from us and chided us for not calling sooner and then asked us to house sit for two weeks while she was in South Africa – though we hadn't even mentioned that we needed accommodation. Later that same day Phillip emailed to say that his apartment was available again. So we stayed at the Consulate General's place for two weeks and then returned to Melrose Avenue, where our LA journey had begun.

20

Or Die in LA

ON THE LAST SUNDAY OF THE year, a terrible thing happened. We were on our way to church that morning when a runaway SUV smashed into us on the highway. It came out of nowhere and smacked into us on the right side – my side – sending us careering out of control at a hundred kilometres an hour. We had definitely not come to LA to die, so as we spun across the five-lane highway, with Sisanda fighting to control the car, I started screaming with great conviction at the top of my voice, 'We will live and not die! We will live and not die!'

We came to a standstill inches from the concrete partition separating us from the oncoming traffic. We were facing the wrong way, into the backed-up traffic that had been behind us but had – fortunately – managed to stop as we lost control in front of them. The drivers' faces were frozen in shock. One or two got out of their cars to check if we were okay, but the driver who'd hit us had sped off, leaving his wing mirror behind on the road, wrenched off during the impact.

I knew God and his angels had been with us that morning, urging my spirit to cry out those words, allowing us to captain our very destiny. My words were symbolic of our greater reality, of my soul's refusal to give up. I believe that words spoken with enough faith and conviction have the power to influence reality. That day showed me a strength within – that I wasn't just a puppet on a string at the mercy of the whims of the universe. We were in partnership with God; he was with us, and we had a strong will to live. Even though things weren't exactly as I'd have liked them, we hadn't made a mistake coming here; it was a crucial part of our journey.

We still made it to church that morning. We were shaken, but not enough to back down. We'd escaped with our lives, our bodies unscathed, but we couldn't say the same for the car. The passenger door had a huge dent, and because we'd taken the cheapest possible insurance, we weren't covered for the damage. After getting a couple of quotes, the car repairs came to $1600. Rita was glad to hear we were safe, but was worried about her car, especially because she'd been planning to sell it, and needed us to fix it. Just then our financial predicament couldn't possibly have been worse and the increasing pressure of knowing that Rita needed payment for the damage to her car caused us much anxiety. We explained our situation, and promised to pay her as soon as we got funds; it was all we could do. But somehow we were always provided for, and miracles of provision serendipitously popped up when we least expected them. When we were down to our last ten dollars, I opened my Bible to read it and six hundred dollars fell out of the book of Daniel – clearly a gift from someone who knew our situation. Moments like these filled us with hope and let us know we weren't alone.

While we were house sitting at the Consulate General's home in Beverly Hills, an opportunity arose for Sisanda to work at the Pan African Film and Arts Festival. Though we really needed financial relief, we were still determined not to earn money illegally, so Sisanda offered to work as a volunteer helping them with coordination, marketing and quality control, a job he really enjoyed. It was rewarding to see him waking up and applying himself to something mentally stimulating and exciting. It helped to keep his mind off our worries.

Whenever there were no castings, I began to sit at Starbucks on Wilshire Boulevard in Beverly Hills and write, which is where this book began. Then, soon after the film festival ended, we moved back to Phillip's apartment. It was comforting to be back on familiar ground. It felt like we'd come full circle.

The castings were becoming less frequent now, but I attended meet-and-greets with more casting directors from time to time. In late February 2008 I had a casting for a film called *Patriots*, in which Forest Whitaker was set to star. My mood was low that day, and it didn't help that a chirpy American actress with a weave down to her butt stared at my hair, smiled knowingly and asked, 'Are you from Africa?' in a squeaky Californian twang.

I thought my audition went fine; it was honest and sincere but with no added frills. As I was about to leave, the casting director stopped me. I'd seen her before at a meeting, where she had teased me about how proper I was.

'You holding up out here in LA?' she asked.

'Sometimes,' I responded, but as I spoke a river of tears spilled out. I rushed away before she could ask me anything else, and by the time I reached my car I was a mess of hot tears. I leaned my head on the steering wheel and wept for quite some time, hopelessness engulfing me like a wet blanket. Tears continued to flow as I drove home. I was nearing the end of my tether. I got word back a couple of day later that I wasn't the type they were looking for, whatever that meant.

The previous day Sisanda had had a very promising interview to work as a runner for the TV series *CSI Miami*. The job seemed in the bag until he mentioned that they'd need to do a bit of paperwork concerning his work permit. When I got home from the casting I could tell he was feeling just as defeated as I was. Hope was rapidly bleeding away, and at times we felt too weak to even offer each other a smile. Every attempt to raise money for our Green Card application had faltered at the last minute; each time the door had slammed in our faces. James Johnson had even offered us a $5000 dollar loan, only for a sudden emergency to crop up the week he was due to hand it over, and he'd needed to use the money himself. I felt like I was missing all the clues; nothing seemed to make sense any more. It seemed that after the accident my mood had begun to deteriorate daily.

In March I met with a well-known casting director, Deb Aquila. Something she said to me caught my attention. While we sat talking, she stopped and stared at my picture for a while.

'The girl in front of me isn't the girl in the picture,' she said.

Not quite knowing what she meant, I said, 'That's a good thing, right?'

'Oh yes,' she replied. 'It's great that you have both these people inside you. That's an actress.' The certainty in her voice resonated. 'I'm a fan of yours, and I'm certain our paths will cross again,' she added as I prepared to leave. It was refreshing to hear this after five months of such uncertainty, during which I'd even started to doubt if I was still an actress.

The next morning, I received a call from Ruth to say that Pearl Wexler, the head of my agency, had spoken with the producers of the Winnie Mandela story. The possibility of this role being available to me had arisen a year earlier, but I'd heard nothing since. They had already signed a well-known actress to play Winnie, but as they weren't sure if she'd be able to lose the weight in time, they were testing the waters to see where I was at and if I'd be willing to consider it in case a replacement became necessary. I had to force myself to not get prematurely excited, as this had always been my dream role and her story was close to my heart. I'd even read her biography as part of my preparation for my role in *Catch a Fire*. And although I knew it was unlikely that I'd end up doing it, the fact that I was being approached and considered for the role provided much-needed encouragement at that time.

Time was ticking away and the curtain seemed to be slowly but surely descending on our dream. Precious times with the friends we'd made in LA became our solace during this time. They would often send us messages of encouragement, reminding us that they were praying for us. I had regular, lengthy conversations with my dear friend Chichi Letswalo, who was in New York at the time, working as a nanny while she studied at a performing arts school. She became my lifeline, and we'd cry on each other's shoulders as we shared our struggles in our treks through the wilderness on our way to fulfilling our dreams.

Sisanda and I now had very little time left before we'd have to leave the country, and our situation was getting desperate. We'd given up much and risked even more to make this work. Despite our growing despondency, we still clung to the hope that everything might change in an instant.

I continued to go jogging in the mornings at a nearby park, endlessly turning the situation around in my mind like rotisserie chicken, examining it from different angles, looking for meaning and trying to piece together the different views to derive some kind of understanding. My will was the only thing propelling me forward; I was determined to find a way. But I kept picturing those who'd scoffed when they heard we were moving to LA. I knew they'd be waiting like vultures, ready to mock, satisfied that they'd predicted the outcome.

My worst-case scenario was fast catching up with me. I didn't want to go back, I'd come too far. But when I looked ahead, I saw nothing but desolation, not even a dancing mirage to keep me dreaming.

Meanwhile, prayer, books, music and writing were my solace and my way of staying grounded, maintaining my view of the goal. But it was difficult to silence the noise of our circumstances, though sometimes, when I fought really hard to find the stillness inside, I understood that things had to be this way. I knew that the dream burning in my heart wouldn't be easy to come by. I was born to live an extraordinary life and I was finally accepting that my journey to it would not be an ordinary one.

On 11 March, as I sat in a state of quiet contemplation, I wrote this poem:

There's light in here
But I can't see much
I can only make out the place in which I stand
Where my feet are.

So many unspoken words between us
Yet when I'm with you I understand
What it all means. But again I look down
And see only where I stand.

There's a design to all this
But I can't figure it out,
I can only see a circle and
I'm in the middle.

So many things you've allowed me to see,
Sometimes I lay hold of it all at once,
Other times I can't feel my hands;
I can only hold all I feel right now.

Hold me forever,
Enfold me in you.
Speak softly to me,
Comfort me.

I started to surf the net looking for a nanny agency, as I had loved the work I'd done with children at Baby Haven and during the school workshops. I knew I'd be good at it – I enjoyed the company of babies and children and had also recently found I could teach acting to children. So I modified my resumé to suit the American job market, and signed up to a number of nanny databases. But most agencies required a work permit.

One morning, as I rested on a bench after a run in the park, I spotted a Hispanic nanny pushing a pram, and went over to ask how I could secure babysitting work. Her only advice, offered in halting English was, 'In a wezzite on a compootee.' Many moons later, once our sense of humour was restored, this line brought on many a laugh whenever problems threatened to swamp us.

The last four days before we were due to leave LA felt like forty days of scrambling in the dark for a miracle. It was a sad time as we began saying goodbye to our friends and acquaintances. I felt numb; I had that feeling you get in your stomach after chewing a piece of gum for far too long, except I was feeling it in my heart. My life was that piece of tasteless gum. Sisanda also seemed to float sluggishly from day to day. Usually when one of us was down, the other would be a pillar of support, but now we were both wiped out, and neither had any comfort to offer; it was God for us both now. In my journal I wrote: 'I'm sick of the waiting, the hoping... I feel bare, stripped, I don't even feel pain right now, only uncertainty.'

Two days before we left, I had a heart-warming moment that shifted something in me. Phillip's housekeeper, Eugenia, had arrived for her usual Saturday-morning shift with her eight-year-old daughter. Eugenia was an immigrant living and working in America, and I'd sometimes helped her daughter with her school projects, browsing for pictures and information on the net. That morning I told Eugenia we were leaving, and as we continued to chat, she asked if she could take me out to breakfast. I said I wasn't hungry, but she refused to take no for an answer. So we went to a restaurant around the corner. It deeply humbled me that this woman, a mere housekeeper – a job I'd always regarded with disdain – was treating me, an unemployed foreigner, to breakfast. Across the table, as I looked at Eugenia, I truly saw her and honoured her humanity for the first time. I became aware that I'd always viewed the world and other people through my opinions, definitions and labels. Now I saw more clearly, and I could connect with these souls, these strangers, and experience home in the most unexpected place. In that moment I felt a comfort and familiarity I'd rarely experienced since leaving South Africa, and yet all along they'd only existed for me as the housekeeper and her daughter. Now, in a moment I hadn't orchestrated, we connected through a desire to touch, love and communicate with each other. It was an encounter so pure, so simple. We were simply human beings, and that was enough. I could finally agree that the best things in life are indeed free.

Finally, the 17th unfolded before us, the official exit date stamped in our passports. It felt as if the past six months had been one long crescendo of tension and struggle, during which Sisa and I had had our share of arguments. Now, in a dramatic climax, we had the fight of all fights that broke the camel's back. It was as if all the events that had taken place had built up and up into a great wave that had finally peaked, and now it came crashing down on my shore, shattering my fragile protective walls.

The trigger was tiny enough. I was on the phone changing the date of our London–Johannesburg flight, and Sisa was busy on his computer. Amid the chaos of orchestrating our exit from the US, we were both completely taken up with our own tasks, yet sharing the silence and the space, a kind of independent companionship I particularly enjoyed. Suddenly he picked up his laptop, left the room and shut the door on me.

Rationally, he had every right to. But something in his manner sparked a flashback to my childhood, where my mother had always locked herself away in her room, leaving us abandoned for days. A torrent of rejection and loneliness erupted out of me. And all hell broke loose.

I didn't, I couldn't, stop for even a moment to rationally consider why he might have left the room. I mean, all over the world, in homes everywhere, husbands leave rooms for all kinds of reasons while their wives are busy on the phone. But the agonising memories of my past rendered me irrational; to me, with no eye contact, no hand signal, he was a man walking away from his wife, a mother walking away from her child.

It felt like he'd looked at me long and thought, 'How did I end up with this woman?' or that he'd finally seen what my mother had seen that made her reject me. I couldn't slow down the frenzy in my brain long enough to grab the reigns of my emotions and steer the ship of my soul. Instead I hung up the phone, stormed into the bedroom and began yelling at him, accusing him of not wanting to be with me, of wanting to leave me.

Sisanda calmly explained his reason for moving to the bedroom – he found it hard to concentrate over the background conversation. How ridiculous I felt! But hey, the rage wasn't about to be turned off here. I'd practised this all my life; I didn't know how to take a deep breath and count to ten to calm my rage and steady my heartbeat. I couldn't unrelease the trigger and bite the bullet back.

In true Sisanda style, though, he began to apologise for hurting me. It silenced everything; those gentle words of his absorbed my rage, my pain, my fire. As soft as rain, they possessed the power to stop my fire-breathing monster in its tracks, like a scene out of *The Matrix*. I could no longer resist this man's love. Yet although the love was right there, waiting for me to fall into its embrace, my feet, my whole body, were fixed as if to a block of concrete. No longer could I turn a blind eye to his commitment to me. I saw it clearly, I knew it, it was certain. But it made me more afraid than ever, because I finally recognised in myself the complete inability to receive it, not knowing how to let him in. It brought me face to face with the truth: I didn't know how to receive love.

But I didn't want this paralysis. I wanted to reject the hold it had over me. I didn't know if there would be any ground beneath me to support my next step, but I was determined to walk away from it, to expose it for what it was.

'It's not you, honey,' I said finally. 'It's me. Something's wrong with me.'

And I broke into a thousand pieces.

Sisanda caught me as I fell. As I wept from a bottomless well, he held on to me and didn't let go. And very gently he gathered up every delicate piece of me. When the flood had calmed to a trickle, he asked more questions, asked me to tell him more about how I felt, what it was doing to me, how he could help – never letting go of my hand all the while. In the safe harbour of his love, I finally unpacked all the baggage I'd been withholding from him, and from myself.

Then, we packed up our things, did our last-minute chores, and caught the evening flight to London.

We landed on the morning of our shared birthday, March 18th, exhausted and emotionally drained. Our plan was to spend a few weeks in London to somehow gather our wits before returning home.

We caught the tube to Hammersmith to meet Simon Bardone, whose wife, Shirley, was an old school buddy of Sisanda's from Union High School in Graaff-Reinet. They'd kept in touch over the years and reconnected again in Johannesburg just before Shirley and Simon got married. Since then they'd always invited us to stay with them if ever we were in London. Shirley worked for the BBC, while Simon, originally from California, was in full-time ministry and served as operations manager at Every Nation church.

The last time we'd seen each other was in Morningside, Johannesburg, when they were on their way to Shirley's family farm to sort out wedding arrangements.

It was freezing when we got off the tube, and we stumbled around lost for an hour or more, Sisa having to keep stopping as he had an excruciating stomach ache. We finally located Simon's office, where we hung around till his work-day ended. I sat reading on a couch in his office, and kept having to jerk myself awake, embarrassed at my drool-smeared cheek. But like a wind-up doll whose batteries had expired, I eventually passed out completely.

Simon and Shirley had a quaint flat in south London, and they took us out to a nearby pizzeria to celebrate our birthday. As we poured out our lament about the past six months, they gave back words of hope and encouragement. A part of me was resigned to the reality that things hadn't worked out in LA and we were now heading back with dashed hopes to a chorus of self-satisfied we-told-you-sos. But another part of me clung to the flickering hope that anything was still possible, to the faith that God could make rivers flow even in a desert.

I still wanted answers, to understand why things had gone the way they had. I questioned God in my prayers and looked for clues and signs to piece together a satisfactory answer, one that would fit into the gaping wound of my soul, even perhaps resurrect my dream that lay gasping its last breath like roadkill on the streets of LA.

We spent the first couple of days resting. We had finally stopped running against the clock, and were now feeling our blisters. Utterly exhausted from the past six months, every bone in my body made sure I knew this. Time spent with the Bardones was balm to our weary hearts. A few days later we went to Dalston to spend time with my friend

Sarah Pasquali, who'd done a splendid job as art director on the set of *Drum*. Originally from Italy, she now lived in London in a stylish loft apartment overlooking a beautiful river. Every morning she made us Italian espresso with an espresso machine inherited from her grandparents. Her world was a kaleidoscope of culture, art and fine films, and our conversations lasted into the early hours. Sarah also had an impressive film library, as her late partner, one of the producers of *Drum*, had been a judge at the BAFTA awards. So with the incessant pitter-patter of London rain in the background, we watched some wonderful films. It was just what the doctor ordered.

But as the days ticked on, my dread of returning to South Africa grew. Sarah wanted to help as much as she could, and organised meetings with some of her friends in the UK film industry. We took a drive into the country and spent a couple of days in Sussex visiting good friends of hers. Carlos believed there was no such thing as enough red wine and cheese, and made the best lasagne I'd ever tasted, while his wife Greta, an actress, was away performing. Being out in the quiet countryside, taking long walks in the meadows and rowing on the river offered just the tranquillity we needed. Sarah always knew what to do; she was a natural nurturer.

The room we slept in had a huge fireplace, and I loved staring into it, watching the flames dance in reckless abandon till my eyes were burning. I'd stare at it as I plaited my hair, tossing clumps of hair from the undone knots into the flames, contemplating the idea that a part of me was burning today in a place I'd never been before, a piece of me going up in flames, a piece already dead.

We were all invited for lunch one afternoon at the neighbouring farm of a lord and his lady, and we passed fine horses and plump sheep about to lamb as we wandered over to the manor. We were a party of about twelve in all, and they presented an amazing spread set out on a beautiful oak table – the very one upon which Winston Churchill had signed the Treaty of Versailles, we were told. It was all fine food and interesting conversation, spiced with a touch of history. But we were clearly the only black people they'd ever had for lunch, and their true British mastery of the art of serene discomfort was flawless.

On our return to London, Ruth called to say she'd be sending a script and wanted me to film an audition and mail it back as soon as possible. I really had nothing left in me for another audition, but who knew what might happen. So we shot it as best we could at such short notice on our small Sony camera. Sisanda directed while reading the lines, an often challenging task for our relationship, as it was hard not to take his comments personally. Once again, my performance was 'good' but I wasn't the 'right type'. By now I understood that it meant I wasn't light-skinned enough and needed a weave.

As Sarah also worked as an illustrator, she had all manner of drawing materials, including crayons, fine liners, fibre-tip pens and pencils, the lot, and I lost myself playing with them to release some of the turmoil frothing inside. It felt good.

I still couldn't quite accept that it was time to go back to South Africa, and big questions kept revolving in my mind. What next? Where to? How to get there? I didn't want it to be South Africa, but reality was staring me in the face. We had no money left and we'd exhausted every other possibility. It was the only thing left to do.

After two weeks in London, we arranged to see the Bardones one last time before we left. They treated us to brunch at the Pizza Hut the day before our departure. The Pizza Hut wasn't my favourite restaurant, but it was a joy to spend time with our friends. As we caught up with each others' activities over the past days and discussed our future plans – or lack thereof – the conversation took an unexpected turn.

Our friends suddenly opened up about one of the hardest battles they'd faced in their marriage. I sat frozen, wide-eyed, as they described Shirley's battle against depression. It had lasted many years, they said, and she had treated it with medication. They were frank about their challenges, and then proceeded to explain how it had all begun – the symptoms and feelings that had plagued her, the random fits of uncontrollable crying and her subsequent treatment.

We sat listening in suspended shock as the conversation unfolded. It was as if, right before us, crooked paths were being made straight so that we could finally see where they led. Answers we didn't even know we were seeking were being laid out in front of us in the comfort of a warm friendship and the randomness of the Pizza Hut.

Glancing over at Sisanda, I finally managed to open my mouth. 'Shirley, I've felt like that every single day for the past twenty years.'

In that moment I saw a snapshot of my soul staring out, sombre and expressionless, from behind a window pane at a raging storm. The London weather offered a perfect metaphor; perhaps that was why London's countenance resonated so deeply with me.

Amid tears and a deep emotional release, Sisanda and I began to ask all the questions that were pounding in our hearts. Their answers poured forth like gentle showers on parched ground. All four of us were teary-eyed by this stage, and very grateful that the Pizza Hut wasn't too busy that morning.

Could it be this simple? My natural guardedness began

questioning the answers. Surely I can do this without medication? Wouldn't medication mean my faith was weak? What would it say about God's sovereignty, about his power to heal?

'Bonnie, if you had diabetes, and the only way to survive was to take insulin, would you?'

After some deliberation, I answered yes.

'Well, this is no different.'

She was right, I knew she was. But there was something else. Taking medication meant admitting that something was fundamentally wrong with me, that I was flawed. I'd be owning up to that haunting voice that had always whispered to me – the niggling feeling I'd walked around with always – that the reason I repelled people, the reason my mother had rejected me, was because there really was something wrong with me.

'We're all struggling with something, Bonnie,' Shirley said. 'Yours just happens to be depression.'

What a moment. My walls were giving way, and I knew it was high time. It had taken so much to get me here!

Sisanda finally got an opportunity to share the burden he'd been carrying in our marriage, the awful loneliness of it. I watched in amazement as Sisanda and Simon silently wept in sympathy with one another. I knew that Shirley, like me, was thanking God for these valiant warriors who were willing to slay dragons on our behalf, yet we resented that we'd put them through it.

Every millisecond of our time together had been immensely valuable. We ended with a quick prayer and embraced as we parted, Shirley offering her ongoing support with any questions I might have in future.

As we waited at the bus shelter listening to the drizzle of rain overhead, we were both at peace, knowing there was a way out of this dark tunnel. What we sought had revealed itself; light had flooded in and exposed the enemy we'd been fighting in the dark. Armed with knowledge, we now had a fighting chance. No doubt the Bardones had already guessed; recognising in my language how I saw the world, and decided to open up to help us.

Not only did the future look brighter, but now so much of the past made sense, so many gaps had been filled in. There was so much to share, we spoke for hours through lots of tears, pouring out the loneliness we'd both experienced in the absence of answers. We'd bridged the chasm between each other's worlds, our strength had been consolidated, we were now united against a common enemy. That night we made love for the first time in a long time, and it was beautiful.

As we left for South Africa the following day we felt closer than ever to one another. The calamity of the past few months had been washed away, and in its place a new feeling of intimacy had emerged. Together we braced ourselves for what lay ahead, knowing that although a big part of the work was done, much still awaited us.

Secretly, during the days leading up to our departure, I had been wracked with the realisation that I'd spent my life trying to run away from home – from myself – in a desperate attempt to forget everything I'd become and build a new identity somewhere else under the sun. And now I was being forced to return to the scene of the crime. As I tried to come to terms with where I was at, I had to acknowledge that the disappointment of the locked Hollywood doors was far easier to bear than my failure to escape all that reminded me of little Bonnie Mbuli.

Anxiety and anticipation wreaked havoc with my mind and emotions. We had left with such hope and were returning now with wounds to lick. We'd left as risk-takers and were returning as statistics. Things definitely hadn't gone as planned, but in hindsight they'd actually gone exactly as they were meant to. Yet how could I explain this without sounding like I was making excuses?

Many questions taunted me on the flight back home, drifting in and out of my consciousness and tormenting my sleep, dead-end thoughts that wound my mind into a maze and knitted my nerves into a pounding headache. How was I going to face those in my life who needed to know? Would they tell me to just get over myself and stop being so self-absorbed? Did I really have to do this? Surely there must be another way? I could always just retreat into my prison; at least it was familiar. I knew how to manage it, after all. Well, barely. What would people think of me? Would they accept me? Would I ever be okay again? Wave after wave of frightening questions crashed on the shores of my subconscious, demanding answers, order, a plan, a structure. But none came.

I'd travelled all the way to California only to discover who my enemy was. I had fled to pursue a dream, and in turn it had pursued me. I hadn't known that the love I'd poured into a dream could turn around and become the elixir that could heal me. All that took place in LA had needed to happen that way. If God had tried to tell me this back home, I wouldn't have listened. I had needed the pain, the desperation, the hunger to force me to pay attention. By stepping into the fire, everything that wasn't real had been burnt away, exposing what it was that I needed to start dealing with.

21

Lost and Found

OUR JOHANNESBURG FLAT was occupied by an American couple we'd rented it to while we were away. In the meantime, we stayed with my friend Nthati Moshesh while we found our bearings. I felt like the walking dead, dazed and confused from the past seven months, wafer thin and as light as a feather.

Our LA venture had taken its toll physically, emotionally and spiritually, and all our funds had been depleted in our futile attempt to acquire work permits that would allow us to get work. It was time to pick up the fragments of our lives and make a fresh go of life. And we couldn't spare much time to figure things out.

Our first priority was to find a doctor and start treatment.

Staying with Nthati was an act of providence; she was not only a good friend but also one of South Africa's greatest talents, an actress who had braved LA herself and had stories of her own to tell. She helped me to debrief and come to a different perspective on all we'd gone through. She reminded me of how brave and courageous we'd been to attempt what we had, and helped me to see the poetic pattern of God's provision at every step. We spent many hours comparing notes about our LA encounters, and it helped me gain new insights. With her help I was able to see that what I'd described as carnage was in fact a constructive path: an essential chapter in the book of my life and a necessary step in my life journey.

Sisanda, true to his task-driven nature, wasted no time attacking the problem of my illness. Armed with knowledge at last, he was unstoppable. I, on the other hand, was still hesitant and ashamed; I wanted to take it as slowly as possible. Where he saw opportunity, I saw impossibility.

'But how are we going to pay for this treatment, love?' I asked.

'I don't know,' he told me. 'But I know God does.'

Taking my hand in his, he asked God to help us find a good doctor, provide money to pay for the treatment, and give us direction through every step of the process. Last, but definitely not least, we prayed that God would heal me completely, forever.

Whenever Sisanda prays, he believes his prayers will be answered on the spot – and they usually are. I believe the same, except for a few occasional questions, like How? When? and *Really?* It has nothing to do with my faith in God's ability, power or willingness; it's because my melancholic temperament wants the full details before I can give full buy-in. Thus far, my encounters with God had proven that he generally gave information only on a need-to-know basis, which I found thoroughly frustrating. When I didn't have enough information or understanding around an issue, I became passive.

As I adjusted to being back I sought comfort from my friends. They, too, were excited to have us back, and wanted all the details of our adventure. When I met with radio and TV broadcaster Lee Kasumba, who generally wears her heart on her sleeve, the compassion she poured out to me across the table broke down my composure and brought forth another fountain of tears.

'What are you going to do now?' she asked. I explained that a social worker friend would be referring us to a doctor, and we were trusting God to provide the funds we needed to start my treatment.

'Bonnie,' she said sincerely, 'I'll pay for it, all of it!'

I dissolved again.

It wasn't just that I was amazed at God's quick response to our prayer and Lee's selfless offer. I was weeping also at my own helplessness in all this. Here I was in need of serious medical help because I was mentally and emotionally unwell, and yet I didn't even have the means to help myself. I had to rely on others to help me climb out of the worst place I'd ever sunk to. Not only did I loathe being seen in this state, I also wanted to save myself, to redeem myself, to cling to this last little ounce of self-preservation and dignity. But here my mess was being paraded for all to see, and I couldn't even clean it up myself. Stripped of every resource or ability to help myself, I was now being forced to fall on the generosity of others.

My perception of the situation was tainted by pride, ego and shame, and I was showing ingratitude before the miracle that was unfolding. I refused to see that my creator had come galloping towards me on a golden horse in response to my call for help; I still wanted it to be me who would save me in my own way. I'd always been proud to be self-sufficient and independent, never needy, but marriage and life had been drilling holes in my armour.

'Thank you for offering, my friend,' I said. 'But I really can't ask this of you.'

'It's okay, Bon. Let me do this for you. I want to.'

'Okay,' I said, 'I'll get back to you.'

What I really meant was that there had to be a better way – my way; a way I hadn't yet figured out. But, given time, I'd definitely find a solution. I failed to see that 'my way' was exactly what had gotten me into this state in the first place. Now I'd asked God to intervene when I had nothing else to fall back on, no Plan B, and yet here I was refusing the help when it was offered. Of course I appreciated it, every bit of it. But I was intent on preserving what was left of my shoddy dignity.

I didn't tell my husband that God had answered our prayer, because he'd answered it in a way that didn't suit me. Instead I decided to wait till he came up with a better idea, like maybe dropping the money out of the sky. That night, as we lay in bed after our evening prayer, my heart began to beat uncontrollably. Adrenalin pumped through my body like lightning, and no matter how hard I tried, I couldn't stop the pressure. I felt like a pot boiling furiously out of control, with its lid about to blow right off. It was physical, I was sweating. I reached for Sisanda, and through gasps for air, I tried to explain what was going on. I desperately needed to control this mounting pressure.

Control, control, *control it!* my mind yelled.

I was having my first panic attack. The last thing you can do during a panic attack is talk, think or take control at that moment. But Sisanda helped me calm down. I'd never experienced anything like it and I was truly terrified. My body was determined to have its say and I couldn't silence it.

The following night I had a repeat attack. It was awful, as though the world was closing in on me and my body giving in. As my gasping subsided to panting, and then to deep, heaving breaths, my beloved said, 'Honey, we really need to get you some help. I don't understand why I don't have God's answer yet. I know he's sent it; I just need to find it.'

I knew it was time to speak up. Things weren't looking good at all. I was drowning, and I needed a lifeboat fast. 'He has,' I whispered. 'He has.'

'What do you mean?'

His eyes grew bigger as I told him about Lee's offer. He was appalled that I could withhold such valuable information at a time like this – and furious. During the argument that ensued, I told him about the shame I felt, compounded by the humiliation of not being able to help myself. But no amount of explaining could wipe the frustration from his face. I owed him more; nothing but the whole truth would cut it. So I levelled with him, unpacking more of the layers, telling him everything I was going through. My whole life I'd taken care of myself and other people; I'd never needed help. Now all of a sudden I found out I was really unwell and had to seek serious help from others, and I couldn't even afford to pay for it myself. I didn't know how to not fend for myself.

'This whole thing is killing me.' I couldn't stop the yarn from unravelling any more, my toys were out of the cot and all over the floor; my dirty laundry scattered everywhere, and I could do nothing to cover my nakedness.

After a series of conversations in which my husband and I both admitted that we couldn't go on like this any more, arrangements were made and an appointment set up. All I had to do was show up and surrender. The panic attacks held off, as though my body was responding to the promise of help and calming itself down, comforted by the hope.

In the days that followed, in one of my conversations with Nthati, she too offered to share the financial cost of my treatment with Lee. I was overwhelmed. God was going to help me whether I wanted it or not, as though a loud message from heaven was booming down at me: 'You need help!'

Lee and Nthati not only helped carry the financial burden; they were also a living sign that I was not alone, not forsaken. They made me feel deeply cherished.

As our doctor's appointment drew nearer, Sisanda kept asking how I was feeling. I felt like such a mess, it didn't seem worth mentioning any more. I was desperate for help. The way I'd been living wasn't living at all, and I resolved to do whatever it took to find a better way, although my fears and anxieties were still there. I detested the control depression wielded over my mind and body, and lived in constant fear of another panic attack. I'd had to make some really tough admissions to myself that could no longer be sugar coated. On 23 April 2008, I wrote in my journal:

Hi, my name is Bonnie Henna and I am depressed. I have been this way from as far back as I can remember. In some crazy way I knew it, but I clung to a hope, a hope that it was all a mistake, a delusion that I could fix it myself – all I had to do was get myself to think, talk and act right. Then eventually I would feel right. I am plagued by the injustice of it all. Why me? How me? Is medication the only way?

Looking back, I recalled times in my life where I'd happened to stumble upon some happiness and was convinced that the hollow feeling in my belly had vanished.

But a few days later that plunging, roller-coaster feeling would be back, always thrusting me to the edge of calamity, making me feel like something terrible was about to happen – to me, to my family and to the world. I felt like the inside of a washing machine, as if I were filled with liquid that just kept whirling, writhing and frothing out of control.

With every waiting hour that went by, it became more real to both of us. This was the first time I was able to share the details in all their ugliness with Sisanda. He always sympathised with me, embracing me as I tried to make him understand, responding with deep sighs of compassion to everything I described. Things began to make sense to him now. He started to piece the information together with the incidents, and would ask questions like, 'Is that why you were so reluctant to give me a hug that time?' or 'Is that why you reacted like that at that moment?' He seemed relieved as all the missing pieces filled in the blanks in our relationship. The mysteries were explained, the memories of hurtful behaviour understood and forgiven. We were both taking our first steps towards recovery.

Our counsellor friend, Sheila Rowe, had made an appointment for us with psychologist Brandon Belsham, who'd recently limited his practice to children and teenagers, yet took me on anyway as a favour to Sheila, who was impressed with his work and assured me that I'd be in good hands. Sheila explained the severity of the matter, and so we were able to get an appointment within two days.

The doctor's office in Blairgowrie was in a quaint house with wooden floors and plenty of sunlight. The glances from the middle-aged black receptionist revealed that she knew exactly who we were – a brutal reminder that I'd soon have to explain my condition to many others, including friends, siblings, my mother and our church folk.

The waiting room was filled with children's books, toys and magazines. The deep, comfortable couch gave me a feeling of safety, and Sisa squeezed my hand tightly as we waited. The waiting room décor brought to mind a lazy Saturday afternoon and the tinkling of the ice-cream van, which was very soothing and helped to ease the tension in my shoulders. Sisa didn't let go of my hand once, and squeezed it every now and then as a reminder of his solidarity.

Dr Belsham was a slender, middle-aged man with glasses, a warm smile and a phlegmatic manner. He kept his hands in his pocket a lot, and his voice was steady and reassuring. Sisanda asked if he could come in with me, but the doctor said he'd call him in a bit later. I was relieved. I needed this to feel like a consultation, and with Sisanda there I knew I'd get too emotional. As Dr Belsham closed the door and invited me to sit down, I promised myself I wouldn't cry. I had to keep my wits about me and keep a lid on things. Just because I had a mental or emotional instability didn't mean I had to carry on like a basket case.

He began asking questions right from the start. I answered carefully, giving as much information as I could. He asked about my parents, my childhood, my work, the inner workings of my mind and soul, my relationships, and an emotional timeline throughout my life up to the present moment, including my physical health. I wasn't able to hold it together as I'd hoped, and soon sat with a box of tissues that the kind doctor had placed in front of me. The slow stroll down memory lane was painful. I hadn't visited some of these places for some time, and never as comprehensively as this. Any reservations I'd felt about speaking and weeping openly in front of a stranger were quickly washed away by streams of tears. Dr Belsham was soft spoken, kind-hearted and non-threatening. His questions were as precise as pinpricks, and he listened with infinite patience as I spilt the beans. He continued to probe gently, and I marvelled at his ability to be so empathic and yet remain objective. Had he heard it all before? I wondered. Was he feeling sorry for me; perhaps even a little bored?

Then he called Sisanda in, and began to explain the situation to both of us. I suffered from clinical depression. My symptoms were enough to confirm this, but he would order blood tests nonetheless. Things had gotten really bad, he said, and the panic attacks were a sign that I was now on dangerous ground. My condition had started out as anxiety but, left untreated, it had later escalated to its current level. The trauma of my childhood had caused so much psychological and emotional damage that, over time, it translated into physical symptoms, and insufficient serotonin was causing my clinical imbalance. He was amazed that I'd lived so long with it without committing suicide or destroying myself through addictions in an effort to numb the pain. It was no surprise that I'd consumed so much alcohol in my early twenties – it was an attempt to self-medicate. He also said it was genetic. Three generations – Gogo, my mother and myself – had suffered from the same condition. The two before me had no way of knowing what it was, and so each had visited great emotional and physical abuse on their offspring. I was next in line. Depending what I chose to do, this cycle would either end with me or become more extreme.

With the silent enemy revealed, Mom's life played out like a reel in front of me. I recognised every one of my symptoms in my own mother; and also recognised glimpses of them in Gogo. All the verbal, emotional and physical abuse Gogo had visited on my mother, my mother had then inflicted on me. Now I held the baton. I could either pass it on or confront this monster and show him the abyss once and for all.

As he painted the picture through his diagnosis, my timeline of events and emotions and their causes and effects made sense for the first time. And now, at last, I began to gain some understanding and empathy for my mother. I saw who she could have been, and recognised that she had always loved me dearly, although it had been masked by the cloud of depression. I understood now where her rage, anxiety and erratic, remote-controlled emotions had sprung from. My heart ached for her and Gogo and, witnessing the carnage in my own life, I could only imagine the pain they had endured without a smidgen of hope. I couldn't wait to let Mom in on my discovery; to let her know that I understood and that help was available.

Dr Belsham could tell, he said, that I had gone through a significant amount of spiritual healing work and counselling through various avenues, but it was really important for me to assist my body in getting back to a stable place. He stressed the effectiveness of exercise, healthy eating and good sleeping patterns. Sisanda and I listened carefully as he gave the diagnosis and prescribed medication, explaining thoroughly why he was choosing Cipralex. I was to take just one tablet daily. Dr Belsham encouraged us to ask as many questions as we needed to. Sisanda asked so many questions that I looked at my husband and realised he'd decided that he too was sick.

The doctor mentioned that he treated more artists and creatives for clinical depression than people in other fields of work; they seemed to have more of a propensity toward this illness. Much to my surprise, he asked if I thought medication would affect my ability to create, as some talented artists used their depression to fuel their creativity.

I understood what he meant. There was a place in that melancholy that had driven me to heights of creativity in my solitude and loneliness; it could be a drug in itself. But I explained that this wasn't enough of an incentive not to take the medication. This would be the true test, then; my talent would have to shine through. If I was really talented, I wouldn't need depression as a catalyst. We kept up our questioning and discussion until every millisecond of our time was used up.

And so my treatment began. If my husband was to be with me all the way – and he was definitely willing – he needed to know what to do, and the doctor had helped him understand how he could support me in practical ways. It felt as though our marriage had been held under water by an unseen hand for a long time, but was now coming up for air. We were finally on the same side, fighting this disease together. There could be no more hiding, I thought. We walked out of there lighter. I could no longer feel that constant pressure against which I'd had to brace myself just to get through each day. We were elated! A new day was dawning, and although there were anxieties, we grabbed hold of hope and celebrated the knowledge that there was a way out.

As we drove to the pharmacy to purchase my first month's batch of Cipralex, I began to worry about whether I'd have to live this way forever. I also wondered if the medication would make feel weird and spaced out – zombie-like, maybe. But by now I was exhausted, I needed a break. I really needed to cut myself some slack; I had no strength to fight another minute.

That day, I took my first tablet. The plan was that I would take five milligrams for seven days to give my body a chance to adjust to the medication. Thereafter, the dosage would increase to ten milligrams per day.

22

Pleased to Meet You

WHEN I TOOK MY FIRST DOSE of medication, I thought, if I feel this good on five milligrams, how good will I feel on ten? I'd never felt like this in my whole life. I was so calm. I was no longer afraid, and the feeling of being watched and chased was gone. I'd finally stopped running. I wasn't a fugitive any more, I had been pardoned. I could get used to this feeling. A slight discomfort at the possibility of getting addicted to the stuff niggled at the back of my mind somewhere, but I would cross that bridge if I ever came to it.

But the first two weeks of taking half a pill made me feel groggy. By now we'd moved in with another friend, Peter, who lived in a beautiful, upmarket three-bedroomed flat in Rosebank. I spent my time resting on the couch, watching

TV or drawing. Everything seemed to have slowed down a lot. It literally felt as though I was thinking slower, as if there was space in my brain, like I was in control of my mental transactions. Colours all seemed brighter in that first week, and my eyes became very sensitive to light. I'd regularly get that dipping feeling of being in a lift or that swaying feeling right before you fall asleep. That felt a bit scary, like I was losing control for a moment. But it soon wore off as my body adjusted and settled into the routine of medication. No longer was I running checks in my mind of my day's doings and conversations, spending hours trying to figure out what people had meant by certain remarks and facial expressions. I couldn't pick up even a hint of anxiety anywhere inside of me.

I was getting to know me for the first time. I was discovering things about myself that I'd only glimpsed in my most relaxed moments. For instance, I actually liked people and was genuinely interested in what they had to say. I was fully and wholly present; my mind, heart and body were no longer being pulled in multiple directions by invisible arms. I smiled more, laughed more and didn't dread the coming day. The fear that had infused my every decision, mood and expectation had disappeared. I no longer feared people, or myself. I didn't worry whether they were thinking horrible things about me, or about what I was saying as I held their gaze in conversation. I no longer suspected that people's smiles and compliments concealed ill intentions. If they said I was beautiful and talented, I believed them; I no longer assumed that they had ulterior motives hidden behind glossy niceties, or were out to swindle something out of me.

This was a whole new Bonnie, and I liked her. I'd known she existed, but now she and I had reconciled. I was no longer divided; a single-mindedness governed my decisions and opinions. I could laugh without fearing that there was a piece of spinach stuck between my teeth. I could enjoy my talent and have confidence in my contribution as an actress, without fearing that it would only be a matter of time before I was exposed as a fraud. Maybe everyone harbours such insecurities from time to time, but my depression had magnified them, legitimised them, insisting that their mere existence proved their legitimacy.

The real me had been submerged beneath a tumbleweed of controversy, engineered in part by the exaggerated stories of how mean and difficult I was, this absolutely unreasonable diva. The aloofness I'd worn as a protective sheath – to keep prying eyes and questions at bay – had made me unapproachable and extremely unfriendly, and this had been taken as proof of my arrogance, snobbery and cold-heartedness. The lethargy and demotivation caused by insufficient serotonin had come across as boredom and sheer disinterest in what was going on around me. Without really knowing and understanding me, those who wanted to appear in the know were forced to invent answers to explain away my strangeness, while I drowned in the sorrow and loneliness of being misunderstood, and the frustration of having no platform to explain myself. And throughout the stage performance of my life, the true me had remained behind the scenes, fighting for her survival.

The industry had lent itself perfectly to my charade; one could feel as small and worthless as a doormat while faking confidence in hot stilettos and designer dresses on glossy magazine covers and popular TV shows. I'd always loved to exercise; this had remained my lifeline, but my body had taken some serious knocks. I'd been skeletal for a long time, as sufferers of depression either take food in excess to self-medicate or they hardly eat at all – my choice was the latter. But now I truly felt alive.

On the second day of my medication, on our way to have dinner with Nick and Sheila, Sisanda asked how I was feeling at that moment.

'It's as if I've taken off my dark glasses and replaced them with rose-tinted ones that make the streetlights dance like fairy lights in front of my eyes.' Now I knew why people called them happy pills. I truly felt happy.

'Wow!' he responded. 'What else?'

'I feel for the first time like everything's going to be okay. I don't see how and when; it's just a deep knowing. I'm hopeful. I no longer want to paint everything black. I'd rather paint it pink!'

I wasn't sure why I chose pink; it was never my favourite colour. Perhaps I'd always associated it with happiness.

I experienced a new stillness. I could make out and make love to my husband without the pull of anxiety to distract me. I could look into his eyes and be fully present with a still mind. My energy was normal again and lasted all day. I was more playful, less wound up, and I didn't take things so personally. Throughout my life, I had always been a seeker of truth, of the most authentic way of living. During my depression, I had immersed myself in God, hoping to be freed of all that burdened me. And it certainly took the edge off; my faith helped me make healthier decisions. If anything, I'd focused quite intently on self-development of every kind; I was interested in anything that promised enlightenment, self-knowledge or growth. But after a while it had felt unattainable. Now that I was on medication, I seemed more able to bridge the gap and actualise all the self-improvement work I'd done. I now had the presence of mind to implement the spiritual knowledge I'd stored up from books, counselling sessions and the inner-healing seminars I'd attended. I'd always had a deep respect and hunger for knowledge, a trait cultivated in me from an early age by my dear mother, and now at last I had the power to implement the social and emotional intelligence it had afforded me.

I was jumping out of bed with a spring in my step. My mind, body and soul seemed finally to be working together and helping each other towards a better me. I now understood what Dr Belsham had meant when he said that healing was a holistic process; you had to take care of the mind, the body and the soul. For years I'd focused only on the spiritual, and hoped this would make up for everything else. But something else was happening. Now that my husband was experiencing a new Bonnie, the sharp contrast between the old and the new made him realise how bad the situation had really been, how much he'd had to endure, and also, how strong he'd been. Suddenly he was carrying less weight on his shoulders, and he was shocked by the transformation he saw taking place before his eyes. I was a calmer, more relaxed and lighter person. He said he no longer felt he was walking on eggshells around me. Getting used to the new Bonnie took some adjustment, and a part of him was relieved that the picture of the woman he had fallen in love with and married was becoming brighter.

But I also saw his anger gradually arise. He was angry that he'd grown to accept dysfunctional behaviour as normal. He recalled all the times he'd known something was wrong with the picture, but had no sounding board or witness to legitimise his findings. He saw the unfairness of it, and I had to hear him out. I encouraged him to tell me everything he was experiencing, no matter how hard it might be for me to hear. And some of what he shared was truly unbearable to hear. I'd put him through so much and he was hurting. He, too, had stopped running after a very long time, and now every bone, muscle and tissue in his body ached. It was bittersweet. We were grateful for this new shot at a more joyful existence, but we were both still hurting. The recovery process would not be a stroll in the park. It was turning out to be a steeper climb than we'd anticipated.

Sisanda also needed to heal from three years of hardship and oppression under which our marriage had nearly collapsed, and we spent hours sharing our painful memories. The most hurtful thing for him had been my distrust of his intentions. I had accused him of not having my best interests at heart; I always suspected him of ulterior motives, and had often accused him of deliberately trying to hurt me. These dreadful moments had really scarred him.

Whenever we'd argued I would aim straight for the jugular and shoot to kill, losing sight of the goal and attacking all his weak points instead. Sisanda is one of the most loving, kind, level-headed people I know, and when we disagreed, he always tried hard to keep it from getting personal. He always kept foremost in his mind that I was his wife and he loved me. He wanted us to come out of the disagreement with understanding, having won against whatever was threatening us. I, on the other hand, having grown up being called names, put down and verbally abused, took all disagreement as a personal attack. I'd never known what it felt like to have someone on my side. If anyone ever had been, they'd never shown it, so I didn't trust or believe him when he'd explain that he wanted whatever I wanted, that he would never deliberately hurt me, and that he would fight for me against anything that threatened my safety in any way.

It was in marriage that I realised I'd never learnt how to communicate. I'd grown up in an environment where sharing hurt feelings was discouraged – you had no right to feel hurt, let alone to want to share it with the person who'd inflicted it. Working through emotional deadlocks and communicating through misunderstandings was utterly foreign to me. I only knew the dysfunctional methods I'd grown up with. When Mom didn't like what we'd done or felt we were guilty of a misdemeanour, she screamed, shouted, called us names or beat us, and we were never allowed to explain, defend ourselves or share our feelings. So that's what I'd learnt to do, and this was how I communicated with my husband. I would either shout and launch a razor-sharp verbal assault and then leave before he could respond, or give him the silent treatment and reject all attempts to build a bridge between us. I knew no better.

Years of these scenarios had wounded our marriage and hurt my husband. Now it was all coming out, and I had to take responsibility for the way I'd behaved. Despite the fact that I was sick and didn't know better, I still had to own my contribution to the pain and the rift that had built up over the years. It wasn't easy.

Neither of us had been perfect, but we were the ones who now had to clean up the mess. We had to apologise to each other for all the harsh words spoken and for the deep despair and loneliness that had resulted.

I apologised over and over again, and he kept reassuring me that it wasn't my fault; that the odds had been stacked against me. Through talking and praying, we grew to accept that although it had been tough these past three years, it was our journey and we couldn't despise or disown it. We could only celebrate that we hadn't perished in the fire, but had emerged stronger, closer and more tightly woven together in love. We both had to learn a new way of operating, and Sisanda, too, had to unlearn all the defensive behaviour he'd adopted. We both needed to let go of certain things, and to embrace, if nothing else, each other.

23

Mourning

ALTHOUGH THE MEDICATION HELPED, I wasn't totally off the hook. I had hoped it would work like some sort of magic potion, transforming all my weaknesses into strengths, turning me into a superhero of sorts so that I wouldn't have to do the hard work of continual growth.

And it certainly did stop the pressure deep inside; it calmed it to a simmer and often to complete stillness. It allowed me space and time to access how I was feeling before my feelings had a chance to overwhelm me, as they'd always done before. The world didn't seem so big and scary any more. My days of being an emotional invalid were behind me now; my emotions no longer ran the show. There was room for my character and my mental faculties to jump in, grab the reins and steer me to a clearing, from where I could make better and more empowering decisions.

The urge to disappear and hide was gone too, which allowed me to be more pleasant to my fans. Until then I'd always found it completely intrusive to be recognised by those who admired my work. As soon as they'd spot me, I'd try my best to disappear, or I'd completely ignore their attempts to get my attention. When fans were rude or asked inappropriate questions, I would feel trapped and overwhelmed, and my reaction would be intense and neurotic. I was also extremely defensive of my physical space, and withdrew into myself like a hedgehog as soon as I felt my space was being infringed.

Now that I was on medication I could greet and entertain my fans, laugh with them and allow them to approach and take pictures. I could trust in the love and appreciation they expressed, and I found amusing ways to field inappropriate questions. I was no longer a victim – surprisingly, in many ways I'd grown accustomed to that role, and had even found comfort in it in the past.

Although I had the medication to help me, I was still fully responsible for the thoughts I chose to dwell on. My soul now had the difficult job of unlearning my old ways of thinking and believing that had grown into towers of habit. I also had to become more stringent about what I ate and how often I exercised; my lifestyle choices would determine whether I had to stay on the medication forever or not, and I certainly didn't want to. My soul became the gatekeeper, standing at the gate of my mind to make sure that no self-defeating, negative or destructive thoughts were allowed to slip in and take up residence, because a negative thought is a stubborn thing; it will persist until it's absolutely certain you're not going to give in.

I'd been a very angry person before my treatment began, and I was still battling outbreaks of it. In some ways I'd grown addicted to this dance of anger, and now that I was working hard to divorce myself from it, it often came back to check if there was still a corner somewhere for it to squat. I also experienced loneliness when I didn't receive the compassion I'd hoped for. Even though my friends couldn't help in a practical way, I'd expected them to understand, especially now that there was an official diagnosis. But some wanted to defy the very existence of such an illness, and others questioned why I was on medication. 'Why are you still taking those things, you don't need them!' they'd insist.

There remained a very real barrier among the black community against any acceptance of mental illness. Most black people I shared my situation with were dumbfounded and frankly very uncomfortable in my presence. They were often just silent or pretended not to hear what I'd said. Some church folk were really supportive, and believed God's providence manifested in many ways, and that he'd given us the brains to invent medicines that could help. But others tried to convince me that taking pills showed a lack of faith in God. I faced a lot of judgement at church, and was met with apprehension and suspicion, which hurt.

I'd have gained more sympathy if my condition had been physical. In black African culture there's a belief that depression is a silly, self-indulgent Western invention; a white man's disease. When life got really bad you had to just pick yourself up and get on with the business of suffering. It seemed that some wore struggle like a badge, and having grown so accustomed to the yoke, life without it was unimaginable.

Weakness wasn't tolerated in our culture, especially from women, even though women are statistically more prone to depression. I often wondered why that was. Was it a refusal to accept help, an inability to accept that they deserved a break from struggle, to believe that if you sprain your ankle in the race of life it's okay to sit out a few laps until you recover? Maybe I had believed that myself once.

I had felt ashamed to admit that I had a mental illness that required treatment, that every day I depended on the help of a tiny white pill just to smile and get through the day. But I was now a fully-fledged believer in the course I'd chosen, and deeply grateful that I'd made the decision. I now had first-hand experience of the vast difference between how I'd felt before and how I felt now, and I could hardly believe I'd got by for so long without help.

After the first couple of days on antidepressants, I stopped asking my husband to be discreet about who he told about it. I quickly realised that the sooner I accepted where I was in this journey, the better my chance of overcoming it and using it as a stepping stone. After that I would freely tell anyone I felt should know, and even began referring to them as happy pills. I caught myself having fun shocking people with comments like, 'I'm so negative and grumpy this morning. Oh, of course, I forgot my happy pills.'

So I was an anomaly yet again. I still felt like I was on the outside looking in, but I was used to it, and now I had to accept that I'd never be like everybody else, whether I suffered from depression or not. This was one of the biggest lessons that came out of this battle. I also had to unlearn my coping mechanisms. I had tried to conceal my sickness behind a masquerade, but the show had to end now. I needed to come out. To do this properly, I had to return to the ruins of my life and survey the damage. I needed to understand what had happened and what effect it had had on me, and on others. And that, unfortunately, was no piece of cake.

Of course, the meds bought me time to count and accept what I'd lost in the fire. But before I could come out and mend things with others, I first had to mourn. I was upset over the time I'd lost, the relationships that had been compromised, the great opportunities that had been jeopardised. I felt I'd been robbed. And I wanted it all back. I wanted to stand on top of a mountain and shout to the world that it had judged me unfairly; I'd been misunderstood. I'd dropped out of tertiary not because I was lazy but because I couldn't concentrate; getting out of bed had been a marathon; trying to distribute too little energy over a day had been gruelling; I'd sometimes had too little energy to answer yes or no; I'd felt dead for much of my life and wished that I was; the media had misread me and I'd been only partly responsible. I'd been ill. I hadn't known what was sucking all the hope out of me, or how to deal with it. How could it all be my fault? I wanted to explain to everyone and anyone that I wasn't and never would be what they thought I was – whatever that was.

Accepting the losses was painful. And there was so much I now wanted to recover. I had badly wanted to study, I loved knowledge more than things. But I'd spent my prime barely surviving, and now I wept for it. All I could do now was take in what was before me, pick up every little piece and move on. I began to accept that I wasn't perfect and never would be; or rather that this was my version of perfection, and that a part of the beauty and mystery of being human lies in the intangibility of perfection.

Something else I discovered as I searched through the ashen remains of my life was my relationship with my mother. I tried to imagine her without the depression. I took stock of her positive traits and realised I hadn't fully appreciated how well she'd fared under the circumstances.

She was one amazing woman. And I began to realise that my strength and tenacity, even my sense of style and grace, were things I'd inherited from her. Our relationship had definitely improved over the years, and having Sisanda as a son-in-law had had a wonderful effect on her. But it saddened me that, although she now had a chance to experience a different way of life by taking medication, I had to respect her choice not to.

24

Under Repair

THE NIGHT OF OUR DINNER with Nick and Sheila, I had mentioned that I'd had a lot of time to think in LA. I'd thought a lot about purpose, and felt a wish to contribute towards developing, enriching and inspiring Africa. In my time of introspection amid the desert of California and my life, my focus had shifted from myself to others, from my own dreams and hopes, to include how I could be a part of discovering Africa's purpose. From a distance I saw her potential, and felt I had a responsibility to the generations after me to develop my country.

I knew there was something I could do, but I didn't know what. I just needed to take a step in that direction. So when I expressed an interest in community development and social reform in underprivileged communities, Sheila asked if I'd heard of the new Community Development Leadership School. The initiative was supported by our church, and due to start in June in Somerset West, near Cape Town. It would involve three months of theory and three months of practical service in the field of your choice.

Both Sisanda and I immediately pricked up our ears. This was just what we needed. We had nothing to lose. Our home still had tenants in it, we were staying with friends and needed to start all over again, our marriage needed some rest and rejuvenation, and I desperately needed time away from the fast-paced, go-getting spirit of Johannesburg. Besides, we had a strong sense that everything was pushing us in that direction.

I also badly wanted to explore other passions and interests. I'd worked in television and film since the age of thirteen, and at twenty-nine I still hadn't been exposed to anything else. The industry and its expectations had dictated the agenda of my life, and I'd built my image, identity and world view from and around it. I wanted to know who Bonnie was apart from the industry. Although I feared I might fall apart without it, I had to go where I feared to. I was a daredevil, I hated anything or anyone controlling or defining me. My journey of self-discovery was ongoing, and my newfound lease on life filled me with fresh courage. I wanted to sink my teeth into something new.

We promptly began organising for our move to Somerset West, and looked forward to its slow, less imposing atmosphere. I felt fine physically, but my body had taken some shots over the years and I needed to take it easy. After all we'd been through we were in need of rest, a kind of sabbatical, but nothing too strenuous or adventurous. So the routine of going to class from nine to five every day felt like just enough to cope with.

A month after my treatment began, we moved. We timed it a couple of days before the end of May, so we could settle in before the course started in June. I was eager to try out my new brain. Sure enough, with more serotonin available, I was impressed at the amount of information I could take in without being overwhelmed. My concentration span had improved and I had the motivation to study and do my assignments.

We were sharing a three-bedroomed flat with a couple who were also doing the course, and it was fun meeting and getting to know new people in the beautiful scenery on the edge of the wine route. Sisanda, meanwhile, started working in the film industry, and ventured into production.

I was fascinated by all I was learning. As the three-month theory phase drew to a close, I found I had truly fallen in love with Somerset West. It also felt like a reunion between me and my beloved Cape Town. The cycle was repeating itself in this place; I found myself recuperating, resting and finding new strength. But then I caught another case of flu, so bad this time that I thought I was dying. The joints around my ribcage also became inflamed, and my chest felt really painful whenever I tried to jog. But with lots of rest, good care and antibiotics, I slowly recovered, despite a persistent cough for another month.

My practical fieldwork of choice was Thembalitsha, meaning 'school of hope', a private school in nearby Athlone for young people who'd dropped out of school due to drug abuse, pregnancy, lack of finance or family dysfunction. The aim was to give these young people an opportunity to complete their matric. Most of the students were over eighteen, which meant they couldn't be accepted back into mainstream schools; Thembalitsha gave them a second chance. This resonated with me, since I felt I'd just received a second chance of my own.

My tasks included running errands for the school, administration, manning the front desk and making sandwiches for the students, since many couldn't afford a packed lunch or proper meals at home. I loved every minute of it and was grateful to be part of something so uplifting.

But my experience was a real eye-opener to the challenges of running an NGO. I got to know many of the young girls, and after a while I started becoming increasingly involved in the details of their lives. I often went home exhausted and troubled – it was so difficult to remain detached from their pain and daily struggle for survival. A few times, I found myself handing them money from my pocket, sharing my personal cellphone number, or lying awake at night trying to come up with ways to help them – and realised I'd become too involved. Though I was doing what I could, their needs were overwhelming and left me feeling useless, and that whatever I was giving wasn't nearly enough to make a lasting difference. The girls were caught up in vicious cycles of dysfunctional behaviour, and facing all kinds of physical, verbal and sexual abuse. Their lives were entangled in an intricate web of relational, material and social poverty, and I cried out to God many times on their behalf. Every day at the school opened another Pandora's Box, and it made me feel guilty that I'd begun to look forward to the time when my practical would be over.

Hearing one heart-breaking story after another became depressing, and my daily dose of Cipralex became my safety net. I often wondered how much heavier the burden would have been had I not had my happy pills to buffer the impact. But it couldn't turn off my capacity to care and to internalise other people's pain and suffering. In every girl I spoke to I recognised myself, my dreams and my own personal fight for survival.

There were some remarkable breakthroughs and memorable moments too. I found a way to raise money for a student to purchase the materials he needed to build a shed in someone's back yard for himself and his mother to live in. I was also asked to speak at the school's first matric dance, where six girls graduated that year. And Sisanda and I had shot a fundraising promo together to help bring in funds for Thembalitsha orphanage's Feed-a-Cot campaign.

On weekends, Sisa and I hung out at Themba Care, an arm of the NGO that took in abandoned Aids orphans or babies whose parents couldn't care for them. We'd help the caregivers to feed, dress and stimulate the babies. It was a world so far removed from the one I was accustomed to, at times I wondered if I'd strayed too far, but mostly I felt certain I was in the right place at the right time. People who recognised me from my TV and film work would ask what I was doing there, surprised at my interest in that world. I couldn't always explain myself and I accepted that.

My community development course came to an end at the beginning of December. Around that time I received a call from the Jupiter Drawing Room, inquiring if I'd be interested in shooting a Christmas advertorial catalogue for Woolworths. It would be short and sweet and pay reasonably well, so I accepted.

I also received a call from a Johannesburg agent, Moonyeenn Lee Associates, which boasted some of South Africa's acting royalty. Moonyeenn was casting for an American series called *The Philanthropist*, which would be shooting in Cape Town in late November, and invited me to audition.

I had pushed the industry to the furthest corner of my mind. A part of me was still raw and disillusioned after my experience, and although I missed it, I didn't know if wanted to be part of it any more. I was afraid that the very reasons I had left to seek greener pastures in LA would catch up with me. My frustration with the South African TV and film industry still upset me too much. I'd given so much of myself to it, and still dreamt of doing great and ground-breaking work, but I no longer knew what that looked like. Somehow I felt I couldn't ignore the bad stuff enough to focus on the work, and that I either needed to stay away for a bit longer or walk away completely.

But when the call came in that afternoon, my heart leapt with undeniable joy.

I couldn't wait for my audition and I excitedly began preparing. The script was fresh and witty, based on the life of a highly successful broker whose life is completely changed after a trip to Africa sets him on a philanthropic course, causing him to seek meaning beyond big money, his luxury Manhattan apartment and his lavish lifestyle.

Once again, art was imitating life. My work had a way of doing that; I had many times been cast in stories that reflected situations or issues in my own life, and through telling these stories I would grapple with the core elements and reach clarity or healing by the end of it.

It was as though God himself was confirming what I so easily doubted, that this was indeed a calling. Mysteriously, destiny had made sure that in the loneliness of my childhood, in the womb of time spent daydreaming and losing myself in the world of books, an insatiable passion for characters, their stories and their motivations had slowly been forged. For me, acting was the embodiment of the truth. In every story lies a truth, and I loved to dig it out and set it free, to give it wings – almost like an act of justice. It felt like a privilege to be able to justify a character's choices and present their story in a way that could make the audience sympathetic to their cause. Through acting I got to tell stories to the world in their most glorious form – without judgement, stripped to their simplest and most human core.

My journey to the knowledge and confidence of calling myself an actress hadn't come about through any one particular event. There had been earlier times in my life when I had avoided it out of fear that if I believed in it, it would disappear and leave me with egg on my face. But every experience and every decision had seemed to nudge me in that direction. And all the while the friction of living was filing away at my rough surfaces to expose what had always been inside me. Now I felt as if this is what I was born to do, and that I had been skilled and equipped for this work in ways that no amount of meticulous planning or strategising could have achieved – as if it was my destiny. I had doubted my acting ability countless times, I had questioned the industry, and I had tried to walk away from it. But there comes a time when the pursued has to stop, turn around and face their pursuer. It felt now it had come time to own the knowledge that I was an actress, and accept the opportunity destiny had presented me with. I had to say yes, I would accept this calling and willingly give myself to it.

I got the part and Ruth negotiated my contract from LA, which meant I'd be remunerated according to US rates for an actress of my experience and calibre, not sold as cheap South African labour to international producers who came to shoot in Africa because they could get everything here at discount prices. This caused an uproar among the South African producers, who were shocked at my audacity. Who was I to think that I deserved that rate? But I didn't cower.

I'd worked my butt off to pay my dues and earn this level of respect. On the hostile streets of Hollywood I had faced my worst fears, and nobody would reduce me to a wannabe trying to earn the industry's approval. I had put my money where my mouth was and confronted my Goliath. If nothing else, those six months sitting face to face with some of the biggest names on the Hollywood casting scene had assured me of my worth, and I no longer doubted my devotion or my ability. I certainly loved what I did and could be relied upon to deliver the goods, but I was going to be paid what I deserved or nothing. Once again, this fed the rumour mill about the old Bonnie. But the difference this time was that I didn't take it personally. I didn't get worked up or angry. I simply made clear what I considered acceptable treatment, and didn't make a show of it. And it worked. They agreed to my fee and treated me with the utmost respect.

Just before I left for Mozambique, Ruth called to say that a casting director in LA had requested me to read for the role of Zindzi Mandela in *Invictus*. It wasn't a big role, but Ruth felt strongly about it because of who Zindzi Mandela was, as well as the honour of working with an industry heavyweight like Clint Eastwood. The audition was held in Cape Town, and I got the part.

Shooting *The Philanthropist* was a dream; the actors were some of the best from all over the world, and the director was also one the finest I've worked with. For the first time in a long while, I was being well treated and paid my full worth, which was refreshing; but this was, after all, an international production house.

After the Mozambique block, our next location was Port St Johns, where we spent two weeks. It rained so much that the production had to be delayed for several days. So I convinced Sisanda to join me while I lounged around idly.

The setting and the accommodation were pleasant and the living was easy. The two of us spent most of our time in my hotel room watching movies and listening to the pitter-patter of the rain.

After shooting was wrapped, we took a restful holiday in Wilderness, a beautiful town strung out like a necklace along the enchanting Garden Route coastline, which coincided with our wedding anniversary on 17 December. By the grace of God, our marriage had roughed it through a four-year storm.

And soon we discovered that I was pregnant.

25

Motherhood

WE WERE EXCITED BY MY PREGNANCY, but not entirely surprised. In an effort to stabilise my hormones after the depression was diagnosed, I had stopped taking contraception. After I started the medication we'd experienced much relief from the hardships of our marriage. We were fighting less, I was much calmer and we both now felt strong enough to take on the responsibility of a baby. The idea excited us both. As we celebrated the news, we felt in a way as though we were celebrating our own strength and that of our marriage.

I continued to take my medication, and when I occasionally forgot, it didn't go undetected for long, because there was still a sharp contrast between how I felt on it and off it. Even Sisanda could tell within a matter of minutes in my company, just by the difference in my body language and facial expressions.

We moved to Cape Town in January of the following year. Our flat on Kloof Nek Road was a dream, with wooden floors and stained-glass windows, not far from the hustle and bustle of Long Street.

Ready as I was to become a mother, it still felt intimidating. My first trimester was miserable. Nausea overshadowed any excitement I felt at being pregnant, and the fatigue pinned me down for almost the whole of the first twelve weeks. How could something so beautiful feel so torturous? I kept wondering. I never got a satisfactory answer, but I was happy to hear that a generous amount of amnesia comes with being a mom.

My follow-up sessions with Dr Belsham now took place over the phone. He had suggested I see one of his colleagues in Cape Town, but I preferred to stick with him; the thought of starting all over again with a new doctor seemed like too much hard work. I continued to take my medication throughout my pregnancy, and was assured that there was no research indicating any danger to the foetus. I was relieved that I now had a better chance of being a good mother; it was comforting to know that I wasn't starting at a disadvantage. But it was tough trying to accept that I didn't have the ability to be a good mom without medication to even out my moods, and that mothers who suffer from depression are more prone to postnatal depression. Dr Belsham couldn't stress strongly enough that we'd need to monitor my progress very closely in the months after the birth.

At times I imagined the worst that might happen to my baby if the medication managed to affect him negatively; at other times I felt guilty for not being strong enough to go without meds during pregnancy. Over and over, I had to surrender to the reality that this was my situation, and remind myself that things could be a lot worse. My gynaecologist reassured me that she'd delivered other babies whose mothers were on Cipralex, and both mother and baby had turned out fine. If this was what was going to help me be a better mom, then this was what I had to do, for myself, my husband and my child.

My second trimester brought more ease. I craved halloumi cheese and ate it almost every day. I was finally enjoying pregnancy. Sisanda was enjoying work on *Invictus* as a trainee producer, and Ruth called me to chat about my role in it. She'd received confirmation of my role as Zindzi, and when she told them I was pregnant, Clint Eastwood had insisted on keeping me in the role. They were happy to shift the dates around so I could do my bit before my pregnancy showed too much, and I did the shoot at five months' pregnant.

A month later, I received an invitation to shoot another episode of *The Philanthropist*; the script had been written to accommodate my pregnancy. Shooting didn't take too long and my colleagues kept teasing me about what I'd gotten up to last time I was on set; they'd worked out that I must have conceived during the shooting in December. And they were right, of course. During the deluge at Port St Johns, while Sisanda and I lay around in my hotel room, what better way was there to spend our time?

In the sixth month, we went for the scan that would hopefully tell us the sex of our baby. We were able to see our baby's movements on the screen, and our little creature appeared to raise an elbow to shield his eyes from our gaze. Then he turned his behind to us, allowing us a full view of his little willy. He was a busy little wonder, and seeing him so clearly during the scan was truly awesome. The idea that a whole person was being created in my womb was endlessly fascinating and humbling for me. I was generally in good spirits and happily preparing to welcome our baby into the world. I loved stroking my stomach while chatting to the baby, to which he often responded with a kick.

We opted for a water birth at home. Through the months preceding the birth, our midwife, Natasha Stadler, shared many details about childbirth with us, three of which stood out for me. First, she believed that while giving birth one walks a delicate line between life and death, neither of which would be fully under our control. Second, through the process I would emerge a changed person, and during this transition into motherhood I would leave behind what was slowing me down and holding me back. Lastly, she said that our marriage would be strengthened by the experience.

God seemed very generous when dishing out marriage-strengthening experiences; we were certainly getting our share. But we could take more, I decided; I'd never heard anyone complain that their marriage was too strong. Needless to say, Natasha was right in everything she shared with us about childbirth.

My due date came, but my baby didn't. Two weeks later I was still waiting. Concerned, I asked Natasha why she thought he was late.

'I don't know, but there's a lesson for you in the waiting, and you should try to find it,' she told me. 'He'll come when he's ready.' It sounded like a syrupy cliché, but she was right. There was more than one lesson there for me, as there always is whenever we take the time to look. In this case, the ones that caught my attention were patience and surrender.

Mom had taken leave and travelled down from Johannesburg to be with me for the final week, and on the final day of her stay, on 11 September 2009, I went into labour.

My birthing process moved through three very distinct phases, and each brought its own revelation. First was the letting go of my fear of the unknown; I had to recognise that there was nothing to be gained from delaying its arrival and slowing down the process. The second involved surrendering to the pain without trying to protect myself. Here I learnt that the pain wasn't a punishment, but its presence helped me to pay full attention and stay present. I'd survived a large part of my life being absent, indifferent and aloof, but now I couldn't get away with that. The third involved taking ownership. I had to accept that I was not a victim; the birth wasn't just something happening to me. I could be in charge if I wanted to; it was I who was bringing a child into this world. These were all important lessons that I would need for the next phase of my journey.

Sisanda stayed with me for every one of those minutes, at times crying along with me when the pain became unbearable and I looked like I wouldn't be able to take my next breath. After eight hours of the most excruciating pain, during which all dignity was lost, our son Micaiah was born.

That moment when I saw my son slide out of me, as if down a banister, was one of the most unforgettable of my life. He smelled of pure wet earth. There was a long moment of unspoken panic as Natasha smacked his bum and shook him, trying to get him to take his first breath, her face pleading for life to show itself. I looked away and braced myself to accept whatever came, while Sisanda began to pray softly. After ten seconds that felt like forever, our son finally managed a lazy cry. Natasha was now suctioning fluid from his chest, and Micaiah grasped the tube and pulled it out of his nose. We all laughed, and took it to mean that he had arrived.

Exactly as I'd been told, the pain and discomfort of the pregnancy and the birth became negligible compared to the joy and satisfaction that filled my heart when I beheld that little bundle of life in my arms. And yes, our marriage was indeed strengthened. My husband spoke of a new respect and adoration for me, and he showed it. As I held my son, a sense of purpose and significance overwhelmed me. The love that bubbled out of me was unlike anything I had experienced before. Its intensity awed me, and I wondered that I had the capacity to love this deeply. It was the kind of love that threatened to rip my heart to pieces if anything were ever to happen to him.

I spoke to him as I had when he was still in the womb, and its calming effect on him amazed me. I could tell he knew my voice. To be known in such an intimate way touched me profoundly. He was so beautiful, all I could do was stare at him, playing with the loose skin on his fragile fingers, stroking his fluffy hair. I couldn't believe he was mine, all mine.

We were very grateful that Mom managed to see him and hold him, albeit for such a short time. A teary softness lit up her eyes as she held him in her arms in reverential wonder.

I cried a lot for the next couple of weeks; almost everything reduced me to tears as my hormones shifted and surged. Sometimes both Micaiah and I cried together, bringing Sisanda close to tears himself, and I was grateful for the safety net of the meds to fall back on. Micaiah is a Hebrew name meaning 'like our God'. My husband and I sat together and looked back in awe at all we had overcome, and we both knew we would not have made it this far without God's constant presence.

During the months that followed, the script of our lives was flipped, and it left us trying to remember what our lives had been like before Micaiah arrived. The change was drastic and we had to adjust quickly. We had known that our lives would change, of course, but nothing could have prepared us for the magnitude of it. Determined to figure out this parenting thing, we just got down to it. And we were doing pretty well until the next upheaval rocked our boat.

Just then, Sisanda and I were offered an exciting creative opportunity to pioneer a film and arts school run by the church. This was a vision that resonated strongly with us, and it felt like a once-in-a-lifetime opportunity.

So we moved back to the winelands when Micaiah was three months old, this time to Stellenbosch. With all its beauty and cultural heritage, Stellenbosch still remains one of the most racially untransformed places in South Africa. This was evident in the three months it took us to find stable accommodation to rent. We were braving one of the most conservative and brazenly racist parts of South Africa. It never failed to shock me how we'd be in a church meeting or a business meeting, and the speaker would switch into Afrikaans without even acknowledging our presence. It was like being in another country. I was reminded of my time in France, where those who could speak English and were well aware I wasn't a local, would still insist on speaking French, causing unnecessary discomfort and prolonging even the simplest of processes, like ordering a glass of wine or a bowl of salad.

The Stellenbosch winelands community was like a well-guarded secret, an exclusive little paradise preserved for the very wealthy. The women looked like something out of *The Stepford Wives*, and their lives seemed narrow and sterile as if they were shrink-wrapped. Sisanda and I stuck out like sore thumbs, braving each encounter, meeting and braai like true troopers, and never once allowing ourselves the laziness of letting others make us feel inferior. This was a tough place; the colour of our skin was highly offensive and we could feel it. Sisanda was better at fending it off, ignoring the stares and the where-are-you-from and what-school-did-you-go-to inquiries. Some genuinely tried to hide their disdain, but others came right out and said – quite matter-of-factly – that they were uncomfortable mixing with black people, as if it were a simple preference between red and white wine. We were left with little option but to nod politely; after all, they were just being truthful.

During this time I made a major misjudgement. Dr Belsham had originally estimated that eighteen months on medication should do the trick, and I had clung to that hope throughout my treatment. Now that I'd hit the eighteen-month mark, I was itching to get off the meds. Clearly, at the time he'd said this, he couldn't have guessed that I would recently have become a mother and undergone a drastic move, thus making it a most inopportune moment to come off the medication. Intuitively I sensed that if I raised the idea with him, he'd strongly discourage it. So after two years of being on medication, fired up with faith and courage brought on, perhaps, by my newfound strength as a mother, I stubbornly stopped taking my meds without consulting my doctor.

I can't say exactly why I was so determined to go off the treatment. A part of it was my desperation to be completely well, a murmuring that had never really been silenced. I had always seen my treatment as temporary, and had tried to speed it up as much as I could in various ways. I had also felt so good and normal for so long, I was convinced I was healed. I was actually starting to forget just how bad I used to feel. So I convinced Sisanda that I was ready to do this, although I could tell he was apprehensive and silently feared the worst. But I figured that even if I wasn't completely healed, I'd gathered enough strength and momentum by now to fight the depression in more natural ways, and that the time I'd spent on medication had given me enough time to recuperate. Sisanda agreed, on the condition that I wean myself off them slowly. So for a week I cut my dosage to half, and then I stopped completely.

I felt fine at first. But like a thief in the night, the depression crept slowly back. A week after I'd stopped, that old, familiar lethargy swept over me, as though my bones were made of concrete. I began losing interest in the things I'd been excited about, and started to get that old, restless feeling of constantly wanting to be somewhere else doing something more pleasing. My language grew more negative and pessimistic, and a slow brewing anxiety was beginning to surface.

Friends of ours, a British doctor and his wife who we'd met in Stellenbosch, were aware that I'd stopped my medication. Noticing that I'd slipped into a downward spiral, they casually asked to spend some time with the two of us, and then gently broached the subject, choosing their words delicately. We both knew they were right, and were grateful that someone had had the courage and interest in our wellbeing to help us recognise what was going on before things spun completely out of control.

I was disappointed that I hadn't made any progress whatsoever. And I realised that I had to now tell Dr Belsham what I'd done; it had been irresponsible not to speak to him about it in the first place, especially knowing how serious he was about monitoring and evaluating my progress. He had never been prepared to even renew my prescription without first having a full session with me.

So I called him and owned up. He was understanding and kind about it, though I could tell he was disappointed. But he was also sensitive to where I was at, and tried not to add more fuel to the fire. I went back on the meds that day, and immediately a welcome wave of calm swept over me, and I was grateful. I had to acknowledge that although things weren't exactly as I'd like them to be, I was fortunate to have the opportunity, knowledge and medical support to do what was needed to be a good-enough wife, mom and Bonnie for myself and my family. And from then on I took my medication diligently with a renewed sense of appreciation, now fully conscious that any slip up during these crucial times would not end well. Micaiah was growing and developing at the speed of light, and I was still coming to terms with the headiness of motherhood. We spent most of the time home together while Sisanda got to work getting the project off the ground. When the combination of breastfeeding, house cleaning and trying to understand Micaiah's ever-changing needs got a bit overwhelming, with some encouragement from my mother-in-law, we decided to get a nanny. We found one through a friend. Elizabeth was a young Zimbabwean who had recently become a young mother herself, and she was hardworking and very patient and loving with Micaiah. This afforded me time during the day to get out the house and back to my exercise routine, revive my ailing social life and try to regain a grip on my world. I also did a lot of work on this book during that time, having last worked on it in LA.

Soon, however, it became clear that our new nanny was in over her head with her own advent into motherhood, as well as trying to get her immigration and work permits sorted out. Sisanda and I helped her as much as we could, at times letting her bring her baby to work. But soon I found

I was mothering both her and Micaiah, especially after her family moved to Franschhoek for work, making it difficult for her to commute every day.

After a year in Stellenbosch battling the language, racial and cultural divides, I felt it was time to leave. The environment had taken its toll on me and, being a new mom, I didn't have the strength to take it any more. All I wanted was to protect me and mine in a less unwelcoming environment. The project we had been trying to start, along with a group of very gifted and hardworking people, had also not taken off as well as we'd hoped; it required far more resources than we had at that point. Thankfully though, we had formed some truly inspiring and dear friendships, which remain close to our hearts.

We found accommodation in Somerset West quite quickly through a friend who managed a group of luxury holiday flats. And immediately, the move brought with it a more uncluttered atmosphere, and being closer to the sea was good for my wellbeing.

We moved in September, a month that seemed always to bring change. The past few Septembers had brought our decision to get married, our first American press tour, our move to LA, and then Micaiah's birth. Here again, as September returned, we were moving home again, aware that our Cape Town cycle was coming to an end. Change was in the air, and as sure as clockwork, it came.

The call came early one morning in the first week of September, as I lay in bed making a mental list of my current goals, which were: (1) to lose ten kilograms to return to my pre-baby weight; (2) to get my mojo back; and (3) to return to the industry I loved. When I got off the phone, I spent a few minutes contemplating the offer I'd just been made in the light of the goals I'd just been visualising. It seemed a good fit, and just the sort of challenge I needed.

So when Sisanda got back from walking Micaiah, I told him about my offer. I'd just been invited to participate as a celebrity in the next South African season of *Survivor*, which was to take place in the Maldives. He thought it was an exciting prospect, and gave it his full support. Without even the slightest hesitation, he said he was willing and able to look after Micaiah while I was away. We sealed our decision with a prayer before finally calling back to accept, and I explained to the production manager that I had a medical condition and could not under any circumstances go without my medication. They fully understood and were aware that other contestants were on chronic medication.

The days leading up to my departure were nerve-wracking. There was a substantial amount of admin, including physical and medical tests. But I spent even more time preparing my mind. More than anything, I worried that I might not be able to handle being out of communication with my husband and son for that long, and I began to wonder if I was doing the right thing. But everything else about it felt right; it had all the ingredients I needed at that point in my life. In his helpful way, my husband decided to test my fire-making skills, giving me a few pointers along the way. To his credit and my delight, I found I could make one hell of a fire!

Leaving was excruciatingly hard. I kissed and squeezed my husband and son for what seemed like forever while my car waited. I still felt I hadn't said a proper goodbye as it finally whisked me away, clinging tightly to my image of Micaiah's cute face and Sisanda's handsome one. It was 15 October, and I was setting off for one of the greatest adventures of my life.

After a few days of settling in, if one could call it that,

the game began. Like many other contestants, I had hoped that the hunger, gruelling challenges and exposure to harsh weather in the game were all staged. But they weren't. We were indeed marooned on an island, and the one who could outlast, outplay and outwit all the others would walk away with a million rand. Aside from giving birth, *Survivor* is probably the most difficult thing I've ever done, unless my memory fails me.

In the days leading up to the start, we waited with bated breath, not knowing whether it was a matter of seconds, minutes, hours or days before the game would begin. Information came to us only on a need-to-know basis. I spent my time trying to work out a strategy, which was futile, since I had little idea of what I was about to face. Then, without warning, it began.

I quickly discovered that all the challenges we see the survivors go through on television – all the hunger, pain, isolation and longing for loved ones – are one hundred per cent for real.

Some days the conditions became so unbearable that the only thing that got me through was that picture of my beloved man and son that I'd clung to so tightly; other days it was too painful to conjure that image because remembering them made me want to give in. Yet through this game, which was in many ways so similar to life, I learnt to appreciate the small things, to live on very little and to appreciate the diversity and uniqueness of human beings.

One of the highlights was the surprise arrival of our family members. I couldn't stop crying and didn't care how ugly it made me look. Just seeing my husband again and having him hold me in his strong arms was all that mattered. The urge to leave the island with him became almost overwhelming. He became teary-eyed when he saw how roughed up I was, which only intensified my extravagant outpouring of emotion.

I fared quite well in the game and was pleasantly surprised at the length of time I lasted. After twenty-eight days I had made it to the top three, and left after the final tribal council on the day the game ended. I walked away that night knowing that I hadn't won a million, but grateful for everything else I'd learnt.

From the day I decided to participate, I'd known there was no guarantee that I'd win, and that it was out of my control, considering all the elements at play. All I could control was my attitude and what I chose to take away with me from the experience. So from the start I'd set three goals for myself: (1) not to give up, no matter how tough things got; (2) to take care of the relationships I formed; and (3) not to sacrifice what I felt was right for the million rand.

And when all was said and done, I could proudly say I'd achieved all three goals. I was definitely a braver and more confident woman when I left, and with the added bonus of having lost ten kilograms in twenty-eight days. I felt a deep satisfaction, the affirmation that I'd had what it took. My first priority on leaving the island was to ruthlessly devour a cheeseburger, so during our stop in Dubai I attacked a big Whopper with cheese and bacon from Burger King – only to be left feeling rather sick. Then I flew straight to Johannesburg to meet Sisanda and Micaiah, who were there to be closer to family and friends for support while I was gone.

Seeing Micaiah and Sisanda was truly heart-warming. Micaiah had grown so much, his features were now more defined and he closely resembled his dad. My heart broke a little when he clung to his father and edged back from me as I reached for him, and I felt a pang of guilt for being away so long. I desperately hoped he hadn't forgotten me. A few minutes later, having gotten over the shock of seeing me after so long, he reached out his little arms towards me. With huge relief I held him and squeezed his little body, with that oh-so-familiar feeling I had longed for on so many cold, rainy nights on the island. My husband shuddered at how thin I was and tried to feed me as much as he could.

Sisanda and Micaiah were staying at that moment with our good friends Caroline and David Webb, who had set up Baby Haven in 2003. Some days after my arrival, while Caroline and I were busy in her kitchen, I happened to ask if any new babies had arrived at any of the Havens recently – by now, two more homes had been added in other areas of Johannesburg.

Caroline enthusiastically described a three-month-old baby boy who had recently arrived at the Adler Haven in eastern Johannesburg. David was busy on his laptop, and she called out to him to open their photo of him. As his face came up on the screen a feeling of familiarity flooded my senses, as though I already knew him. I not only saw him as the boy in the picture, but as the person he would be in years to come. As I stood there staring at his image on the computer, a knowledge that he belonged with us settled peacefully in my heart, and my head seemed to silence all opposing reason.

I thanked David and walked over to the flatlet on their property where we were staying where I told Sisanda that I thought we'd met our new son. He didn't seem too shocked, and took my hand to pray, asking God for guidance and wisdom to help us make the right decision.

Years earlier, the seeds of adoption were already sown in my heart when I started volunteering at Baby Haven before I met Sisanda. I'd made a silent promise to myself that one day, when I had a healthy and functional family environment in which to raise one of these little ones, I'd adopt without hesitation. After our marriage, when Sisanda had often joined me with the babies, I could tell from his tenderness with them that adoption was something he'd consider. He'd later said as much.

That evening, over dinner with David and Caroline, we told them that we knew we were to parent this baby. They were pleasantly surprised, and David showed Sisanda the picture of his new son on the computer. It felt so surreal, especially after my life-changing experience in *Survivor*. I had barely been back a week, and here I was, taking on yet another mammoth challenge.

As Sisanda and I chatted about our decision, we realised that somehow, over the years, everything we'd gone through had only served to make us even bigger risk-takers, and we marvelled at it. After a few misses, it would have been reasonable for us to be more cautious about risk, yet we had emerged even more brazen than before. Past failures hadn't managed to dampen our spirits, and we seemed destined to live pioneering, out-of-the-ordinary lives.

We contacted the social worker the following day, who explained the process. First, we needed to go through a screening process to approve us as foster parents. We'd also need to take the baby for medical tests and get his clinic card. I was still exhausted and busy readjusting to normal life after *Survivor*, and Micaiah was now a demanding toddler, so Sisanda's sharp admin skills came in very handy. Within a week we had little Hanniel with us, ready to travel back with his new family to his home in Cape Town.

I had barely had time to get my head around the idea of having a three-month-old baby in the house, and had brief moments of panic wondering if we'd acted too hastily. I sincerely hoped we'd done the right thing. But I was consoled by the knowledge that Hanniel needed a loving home, and we could give him that. Everything else could be figured out as we went along. All I knew for sure was that he belonged with us. There were many adjustments to be made, but luckily, Micaiah's infancy wasn't so far behind us, so we weren't completely out of practice.

Micaiah didn't seem to understand that Hanniel was an infant, and constantly tried to get a reaction out of him. Some of Micaiah's attempts included lying on top of him, throwing a toy at him and pulling at his cheeks or other parts of his face, so we couldn't leave Hanniel alone with him for a second. It became a running joke that Micaiah was now a baby basher. But he quickly outgrew that phase and became territorial instead, realising that he now had to share his parents with a sibling. He found a way to reclaim the spotlight by crying whenever one of us held Hanniel, and pretending to cry whenever Hanniel cried so that he too could be picked up.

But that phase didn't last either, and finally he couldn't resist falling in love with Hanniel. He started being affectionate and protective of his little brother, and Hanniel, in turn, adored his big brother.

There was, naturally, some surprise when Hanniel joined us. 'I never guessed you were pregnant!' people said, or 'Wow, you've had your boys so close in age!' We simply responded with a polite yes or a nod, and only explained to close friends and family. I especially enjoyed the comments about how great my body looked after two babies!

But Hanniel's first weeks with us weren't easy. He and I were still bonding and getting to know each other, and often he seemed to push me away and reject my advances. He warmed much more readily to Sisanda, but with time our interactions became easier and more comfortable. Looking at Hanniel, I couldn't help feeling that he had an awesome destiny ahead of him, and I decided that this was one of the reasons God had orchestrated such a distinct intervention. As time passed, Micaiah and Hanniel grew inseparable, and Hanniel mimicked everything Micaiah did. Ironically, Hanniel and I are similar in many ways, and watching him grow and getting to know him has taught me a lot about myself.

Our journey with Hanniel has also led us down new paths. I've become the current spokesperson for Adoption Voice SA, and we've done many media interviews to tell our adoption story. This has encouraged many other families to consider adoption, and raised awareness of the many children left orphaned by the scourge of Aids. It's a call to action for all South Africans to solve this problem in our own back yard. A handful of Hollywood actors cannot solve this, and the problem isn't theirs to solve. We can make a difference and do it ourselves. In the words of the African proverb, it takes a village to raise a child.

When we returned to Cape Town that December, we could feel that something had shifted. It was apparent to both of us that our time in Cape Town had come to an end. I was itching to get back to work, which trickled in too slowly. All our work prospects seemed to be leading us to Johannesburg. As hard as it always was for me to leave Cape Town, I realised that staying longer than we needed to wouldn't be constructive for any of us.

I cried for a good two hours of the drive back to Johannesburg in January 2011. And yet, for the first time in my adult life, Johannesburg felt like home. The pressure I'd always associated with it was gone, and it felt like a fresh start. And deep in my heart, after all my restlessness and constant relocations, I felt it was time to settle down, to lay down roots and let them grow deep and strong.

Epilogue

THE INDUSTRY I LOVE welcomed me back with open arms. And now that I've learnt how to allow myself to be loved, I've been blessed and deeply healed by the warmth and appreciation of my fans. For the media, it might seem as though they're meeting me for the first time. Publicity is something one grows to understand and manage with time. It's not a destination but a by-product, which can either become a lethal addiction or a means to influence society positively. I'm deeply grateful for the platforms it has presented me with to share ideas and thoughts that may hopefully provide clues to a more fulfilling life, especially for young women.

I still take my happy pills, and I'm extremely thankful for

the second chance they've given me to enjoy all the beauty in my life. I've come a long way: my medication has changed to Zoloft, and my dosage has reduced from one and a half pills to half a pill. I don't know when, but the time may come when I no longer need medication. Until then, I'm grateful to take what I need each day. But I've also had to accept the possibility that I may never get off medication. Whatever this might mean I honestly don't know, but I've opened my heart to that possibility, and arrived at the perspective that it doesn't in any way rob me of a hopeful and exciting view of my future.

When I first got married, I feared that my wings would be clipped, and that being a wife and a mother would deprive me of the adventure I longed for. It hasn't. Instead, I know that life has packaged for me the most spectacular adventure: the discovery of the real Bonnie Henna. It's a daily treasure hunt and will remain so for the rest of my life. On the other hand, my ever-present longing for adventure continues to be fed by all the risks I've taken and all those that are still to come. I've grown to value life's unpredictability.

I have also been able to mend bridges with my beloved mother. Becoming a mother myself has opened up a whole new understanding of her challenges and the position she found herself in all those years ago. I'm proud of who I've become, and a large part of that is through her doing and sacrifice. It warms my heart to see my mother with her grandchildren, because in a sense she too has received a second chance to be the mom she always was beneath the rubble of her own heavy pressures.

Three generations of women in my family have fought the same monster called depression. I believe I have defeated this Goliath forever, not only in my own lineage, but in countless others through this sharing of my story.

And God, who started out for me as a distant watcher guy, is now my ever-present companion, inching closer to me with every passing day. I no longer feel like a helpless pawn in his game. I play my own part in my moves on the chessboard of life.